RUSS ALAN PRINCE • DO　　　　　　　　　　　　S, JR.

Accountants as Wealth Managers

THE NEW PARADIGM FOR PROVIDING FINANCIAL SERVICES

Accountants as Wealth Managers: The New Paradigm for
Providing Financial Services

Russ Alan Prince, Douglas D. Wright, and Richard C. Urbealis, Jr.

Institutional Investor News
225 Park Avenue South
New York, NY 10003
1-212-224-3800
www.iinews.com
www.iihighnetworth.com

Additional copies of this publication may be obtained by calling
1-212-224-3800 or sending an email to: customerservice@iinews.com.

ISBN number 1-893339-83-1

To those who are forcing me to live where the trees move.

RUSS ALAN PRINCE

*To my two sons, Collier and Andrew, who have been my
inspiration for 13 and 15 years.*

DOUGLAS D. WRIGHT

*To my wife Kyle, who makes me want to be a better man and
to my four children who give me great joy and happiness.*

RICHARD C. URBEALIS JR.

Table of Contents

Foreword:
Welcome to the New Paradigm

The financial services world is upside down.

At one time, it was an orderly and predictable place. Brokers handled stock. Insurance agents sold life insurance. Bankers made loans. Lawyers designed estate plans. And accountants took care of the taxes. No longer. Financial services firms have been rethinking the way they work with their affluent clients. As a result, brokers offer every imaginable financial product and service. Insurance agents provide estate planning. Banks routinely offer insurance and brokerage services. And law firms are setting up joint ventures to create trust departments and money management operations.

In the midst of this change, accounting firms are also reconsidering their business approach. Firms have to decide whether they want to stay with the traditional model of providing accounting and tax services, add a financial services component by selling some financial products, or move to an entirely new model of wealth management that delivers a total client solution.

There are a number of factors driving this change in the financial services world. First, there have never been as many wealthy Americans as there are today. Even with the recent recession, the *Merrill Lynch/Cap Gemini Ernst & Young World Wealth Report 2002* reported that the number of Americans with at least $1 million in investable assets actually rose in 2001.

Secondly, thanks to such factors as the Internet and CNN, the affluent are more aware of their financial options than ever before. And while that awareness is increasing, most affluent individuals look to their financial advisors to fill gaps and make recommendations. According to Nationwide Financial's recent study of high income investors, the affluent know the least about the financial products designed to meet their stated goals.

Finally, the more money people have, the more complex their financial situation becomes, so they want a wealth management solution that covers every aspect of their financial life. According to Nationwide Financial's study, the affluent are looking for financial plans, income management in retirement, investment risk and return analysis, tax advice, and estate planning services.

This book is based on the authors' research into the nature of the paradigm shift in financial services – and how those in the accounting industry can respond to it and benefit from it. The authors considered the pros and the cons of the move to wealth management and demonstrate a number of compelling reasons to move to this kind of model, including deeper client relationships, increased profitability through cross-selling, and more referrals.

Making such a change is quite a leap. At the same time, there is a sense of urgency because it's hardly a secret that wealth management is the way to go. It seems as if every financial firm is trying to get into wealth management business through acquisitions, alliances, or ad campaigns that position them as the advisor of choice.

In that competitive mix, we agree with the authors, who believe that the accounting industry has some important assets that set it aside from other financial advisors. Clearly, accountants are well positioned to make the shift to wealth management. Our research at Nationwide Financial tells us that 93 percent of the affluent report using an accountant in some capacity and 50 percent report turning to their accountant for financial planning help. Most accounting firms have well-established and longstanding working relationships with their clients, for instance, that have led to a high level of trust that's not typical of many other advisory relationships.

In addition, despite the recent travails of Arthur Andersen, the accounting profession is still very well regarded by the affluent. Our research tells us that the vast majority, 85 percent, of affluent individuals who work with accountants say that these situations have not eroded their trust in these advisors. And our research complements the authors' research, which shows that the affluent are very open to the idea of relying on their accounting firms for other financial services – of seeing those firms as not just accountants, but wealth managers. This is what the paradigm shift is all about.

In this book, the authors demonstrate why they feel change should be made and how it can be done. Nationwide Financial believes that accounting firms across the country will choose this kind of approach. Those that are ready to change can enter a new paradigm and provide a full range of wealth management solutions for their clients.

Robert Rolland, Vice President
Nationwide Financial Services, Inc.

July, 2002

Executive Summary

A paradigm consists of the concepts and definitions that go into a generally accepted theory. A paradigm shift occurs when one paradigm is exchanged for another. As the accounting profession is evolving into financial services and wealth management, a paradigm shift is occurring that's taking the industry from its traditional model of accounting as separate from other financial service to a wealth management model where accountants deliver the full range of accounting, investment, planning, and insurance services to affluent clients in a consultative manner.

There are three stages of the paradigm shift model for accountants. They are: *Stage 1: The "Traditional" Accountant* (this is the current paradigm through which accountants offer basic accounting and tax services); *Stage 2: The Accountant as Financial Advisor* (this is the transitional stage during which accountants provide basic accounting and tax services and also begin to sell financial products), and *Stage 3: The Accountant as Wealth Manager* (this is the new paradigm, during which accountants provide basic accounting services while also delivering a full range of financial products and services is a consultative manner).

STAGE 2: **The Accountant as Financial Advisor**

CHAPTER 3: Providing Financial Services ....page 31

Our research showed us that nearly one out of every five CPA firms had already reached *Stage 2* and nearly half of the remaining firms expected to be offering financial products and services in the next three years.

CHAPTER 4: The Financial Services Opportunities
for Accountants ....page 43

Individuals and small business owners who already obtain financial services from accountants are very satisfied with both the quality of the products and the level of service they receive. There's also considerable interest in financial services among clients who don't currently get them from their accountants.

CHAPTER 5: Critical Success Factors in
Financial Services...page 59

The top three critical success factors cited by those CPA firms that have successfully entered the financial services field are: 1) having partners identify prospects for the financial services practice, 2) creating strategic alliances with experts in life insurance and investments, and 3) being able to access financial services professionals on a case-by-case basis. Firms that have entered but then exited the financial services business offered three main reasons for their failure: 1) the firm was never fully committed to the business, 2) implementation was problematic because there was not a change "champion" among the partners, and 3) there were conflicts with the firm's financial services provider(s).

STAGE 3: The Accountant as Wealth Manager

The wealth management platform combines disciplines – traditional accounting, investment management, and advanced planning – and delivers them in a highly consultative manner. Though few accounting firms have evolved to this stage, adopting the wealth management model has been demonstrated to increase revenues and profitability in the private banking, life insurance, and brokerage industries.

The specific steps to building the wealth manager platform are: 1) conduct an internal assessment (including a critical evaluation of the client base), 2) evaluate and select one of the four business model alternatives (Build, Buy, Joint Venture, or Referrals), 3) build the wealth management infrastructure, and 4) establish an expert support structure.

A successful transition to the new wealth management paradigm hinges on paying strict attention to critical success factors, including having one partner in charge, creating the right infrastructure, building alliances with experts in investment management and advanced planning, and ensuring that firm members can readily access that expertise.

List of Exhibits

STAGE 3: The Accountant as Wealth Manager

Stage 1

CHAPTER 1

The Nature of Paradigms

"Turbulence is life force. It is opportunity. Let's love turbulence and use it for change."

RAMSAY CLARK

Executive Summary

A paradigm consists of the concepts and definitions that go into a generally accepted theory. A paradigm shift occurs when one paradigm is exchanged for another. As the accounting profession is evolving into financial services and wealth management, a paradigm shift is occurring that's taking the industry from its traditional model of accounting as separate from other financial services to a wealth management model where accountants deliver the full range of accounting, investment, planning, and insurance services to affluent clients in a consultative manner.

The role of the accountant is changing. In the context of financial services, the changes in the accounting profession are so sweeping that they can seem unprecedented. They're not. There are not only many examples from other industries, but there's a scientific term for such change processes: a paradigm shift.

Human affairs go through a paradigm shift when one way of thinking gives way to something quite shockingly new. We contend that the business of accountants, particularly those catering to affluent private clients and small to mid-sized businesses, is currently undergoing such a paradigm shift.

In this chapter we'll discuss how that is happening. First we'll consider the concept of the paradigm and then examine a paradigm shift. Finally, we'll look at the nature of the paradigm shift in the world of accounting as it relates to the financial services industry.

What Is a Paradigm?

The idea of a paradigm grew out of the social sciences of the 20th century. Social sciences sought to explain how people think about their world, how they organize their experiences into frameworks, and how people decide what is (or is not) "real." This search for how people think about knowledge (what they "know") permeated a field called the history of science, which is the study of how scientists "know" science.

What they began to discover was that in any one era, one way of thinking would be generally accepted. It would be accepted so widely that it was never questioned. It was "true." The classic example of this is that for several thousands of years people believed that the sun rotated around the earth. The "fact" that the sun and stars and the whole universe rotated around the earth was universally accepted and believed. It was not open to question.

A historian of science named Thomas Kuhn coined the term "paradigm" for this kind of thinking. He wrote a book called *The Structure of Scientific Revolutions* that spelled out his ideas about paradigms. According to Kuhn, "a paradigm is global idea embracing all the shared commitments of a (scientific) group." A paradigm, according to Kuhn, consists of the laws, rules, models, concepts, and definitions that go into a generally accepted, fundamental theory of science. A paradigm is the web of accepted theories through which scientists normally regard their subject. Such a paradigm is global in character.

The Greek roots of the work paradigm are the prefix *para*, for "alongside," and the root *deik*, for "show" or "teach." The idea is that a paradigm is something that explains other things. In this way, a paradigm is related to ideas like "pattern," "structure," "formula," or "model." But it's generally used to refer to the largest of these ideas, to the ideas that are the most basic to all of human thinking.

What Is a Paradigm Shift?

Kuhn created this idea of a paradigm because he wanted to explain a concept that was even more compelling – the paradigm shift. A paradigm shift occurs when one global paradigm is replaced by another.

Let's go back to the paradigm of the sun rotating around the earth. That was the existing paradigm for most of human history. We no longer believe it because Galileo took out a telescope and saw the moons of Jupiter. Galileo (and others) did enough good science to prove to other scientists that the earth goes around the sun, as do the other planets. This idea was a whole new paradigm. In a relatively short period of time, one basic elemental idea of "how things are" was replaced by a completely different idea of "how things are." This is a paradigm shift.

Here's another example of a paradigm shift, also taken from science. Remember that by Kuhn's definition, a paradigm is a set of inherited preconceptions, the lens through which we habitually view the world. When someone shatters the lens (as Einstein did with his theory of relativity) everyone is forced to ask questions differently and to view the challenges of science and philosophy in a new way. The swift transition from Newtonian physics to Einsteinian physics is another example of a paradigm shift. This idea of a paradigm is such a valuable idea that it's spread throughout the vocabulary of the social and natural sciences, philosophy, art criticism, and business management. This idea has been very useful to explain the rapid changes in thinking that have to accompany the dynamic changes in the world. Now people use the paradigm and paradigm shift concepts to describe phenomena far afield from physics and science. There is now a "welfare paradigm," a "hospital paradigm," the "12-step paradigm," "urban paradigms," and "market paradigms." People who call for a change in the "educational paradigm" behind employment training are arguing that such training should not be done by schools, or even in classrooms. In seeking a "new leadership paradigm," a trade group is calling for new forms of leadership and new management styles.

But what has all this to do with accounting and financial services?

Paradigm Shifts and the Financial Services Industry

There is a compelling reason to understand the concept of a paradigm shift because one is going on right now in the world of accountants.

What is the accepted, traditional, paradigm in the accounting profession?

Like scientific systems, accounting systems have been used for thousands of years. As businesses grew, accounting systems were invented by people to keep track of costs, profits, and losses. Modern accounting measures and communicates financial information about an economic entity. This information is used to plan, control, evaluate, and make decisions about a business. The process begins with bookkeeping, which records transactions such as checks and invoices and summarizes these transactions in financial statements. Financial managers use the financial statements to raise and spend cash and to make intelligent financial decisions. Accounting is the information system that measures, processes, and communicates financial information about an identifiable economic entity.

The traditional accounting paradigm is that accounting is separate from other financial services industries. The traditional paradigm is that accountants were separate from bankers, insurance agents, brokers, and financial advisors. This paradigm was reinforced by legislation that mandated the separation of these sectors and by professional ethical standards (Exhibit 1.1).

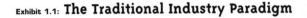

Exhibit 1.1: **The Traditional Industry Paradigm**

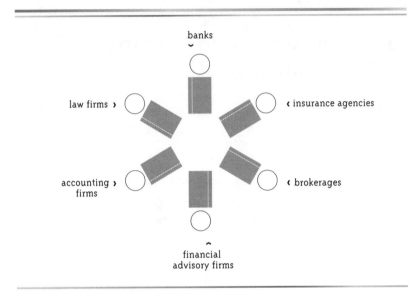

In the traditional paradigm, bankers took cash and paid interest and made loans. Brokerages invested money for clients. Insurance agencies provided vehicles to hedge against various sorts of risk. Accounting firms collected and reported financial information. Law firms created contracts and other legal documents and provided advice on laws and regulations. Financial advisory firms performed financial planning for their clients.

This is changing. There is a new industry paradigm (Exhibit 1.2). In the new paradigm, each of these separate entities is now invading each other's space. Banks now sell insurance and manage investments for their banking customers. Brokerages routinely offer the trust services that used to be the bank's home turf. Insurance agents are selling investment management services and doing the kinds of planning once done by accountants and financial planners. Financial planners now provide insurance and investments and are making strategic alliances with banks. And law firms are now getting into these businesses as well.

EXHIBIT 1.2: **The New Industry Paradigm**

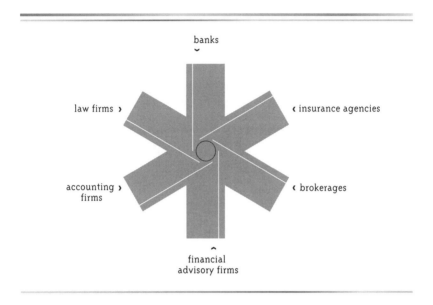

Let's look at the traditional and new paradigms from the client's point of view. Imagine that the client is a female and the owner of a small business. She has the usual financial management needs for her business. According to the traditional paradigm, the client would have her accounting firm assist with the accounting and tax needs of the business and her personal life and with tax preparation. She would go to her financial advisor for help on estate planning. She would call on her attorney to draw up a will and trust documents and for other legal needs. The insurance agent would help with some of the benefits planning for the company and with personal insurance needs. She would go to her broker for investment products. According to the traditional paradigm, clients are often the "systems integrator," the ones responsible for pulling together all the aspects of their (financial) life. The traditional paradigm was one of "specialists."

In another version of the old paradigm, accountants may act as advisors across the system; often at the side of the client when working with other business advisors.

The paradigm shift is where accountants directly enter the financial services business. It is where they first became financial advisors – the transition stage in the evolutionary cycle. Operationally, this is where the accountant sells investments and insurance products for fees or commissions. At one time this idea was heretical just as the idea that the earth was not the center of the universe. Now, everyone within the accounting industry, financial services institutions, and a great many clients readily accept this world view.

There are extensive limitations to the accountant as financial advisor; limitations that can be overcome as the new paradigm gets increasingly refined. This evolution can be summed up in the phrase, "focused one-stop shopping." The next step in the evolution of the paradigm is to build the single relationship through which clients can obtain potentially extensive but selected financial services and products for their comprehensive financial management; in effect wealth management.

In this paradigm, aside from the core services characteristic of CPA firms, the carefully chosen financial services are sourced from whichever entity provides the greatest value. The key is that integration is provided by a firm of the client's choosing. This firm integrates the services of all the other firms and is compensated as the other firms would be compensated. Moreover, this integrated set of financial solutions is delivered in a highly consultative manner.

In the evolved paradigm, the goal of the accounting firm is to be the integrating firm – the wealth manager. The difference between the paradigm as it is today, the financial advisor, and the advancement that is just now becoming apparent, the wealth manager, is much more than terminology. While a cursory examination shows us that the products and services are very often the same, wealth management is a very different way of working with clients. It is a holistic approach which actually best suits the situation accountants tend to find themselves in. Thus, wealth management – while part of the paradigm shift – is an evolutionary conclusion. And it would not be possible without the starting point of the financial advisor.

Strategic Considerations

The industry is in the process of changing. It doesn't matter whether or not this change is welcome. The change is happening.

What does matter is the way that accountants and accounting firms respond to this change. The objective of this book is to help them understand and manage change.

CPA firms can use the questions in Exhibit 1.3 to audit their firm's strategic context and situation. First, consider the major changes taking place in the accounting profession and the financial services industry. We have been focusing on the convergence taking place within the financial services industry. Will the accounting industry change the same way and at the same pace? Next, what evidence is there of the emergence of cross-disciplinary selling and provisioning of financial services (the new paradigm)? Is there evidence of this among the firm's competitors and clients? Finally, consider what the firm's response should be.

EXHIBIT 1.3: **Auditing a Firm's Strategy**

Focus Topic	Comments
What are the major changes impacting the accounting profession and the financial services industry?	
What evidence is there of the emergence of cross-disciplinary selling and provisioning of financial services (the new paradigm)?	
In broad terms, what will the firm's response be?	

CHAPTER 2

An Evolution: From Accountants to Wealth Managers

"They always say that time changes things,
but you actually have to change them yourself."

ANDY WARHOL

Executive Summary

There are three stages of the paradigm shift model for accountants. They are: *Stage 1: The "Traditional" Accountant* **(this is the current paradigm through which accountants offer basic accounting and tax services);** *Stage 2: The Accountant as Financial Advisor* **(this is the transitional stage during which accountants provide basic accounting and tax services and also begin to sell financial products), and** *Stage 3: The Accountant as Wealth Manager* **(this is the new paradigm, during which accountants provide basic accounting services while also delivering a full range of financial products and services is a consultative manner).**

We're all familiar with the traditional paradigm for accounting firms: providing core accounting services to clients. To do that, CPAs educate and organize themselves to serve the reporting, tax, and business interests of their clients. They provide, for instance, industry data and analysis so that business owners can make informed decisions.

Now we're noticing that the paradigm is beginning to shift (Exhibit 2.1). It's getting increasingly difficult for many CPA firms to grow and be highly profitable by only providing accounting services. As a result, many of those firms have started to augment the portfolio they offer their individual and business clients with financial products such as insurance and investment products such as annuities, mutual funds, and managed money. In our model, this move corresponds to *Stage 2: The Accountant as Financial Advisor.*

Stage 2, however, should be seen as transitory, nothing more than a halfway point between two stages that are highly stable (if very different in terms of their scope and profit potential). Merely adding financial products and services is not enough if the goal is to best serve clients and maximize opportunities for profit. Accountants and accounting firms should therefore continue to transform themselves and become fully integrated, consultative services providers. This new paradigm is the wealth management model that we call *Stage 3: The Accountant as Wealth Manager.*

EXHIBIT 2.1: **The Stages in Development of an Accountant's Business Model**

STAGE 1: The "Traditional" Accountant	Old paradigm	Core accounting and tax services.
STAGE 2: The Accountant as Financial Advisor	Transitional stage	Core accounting and tax services, as well as the selling of financial products.
STAGE 3: The Accountant as Wealth Manager	New paradigm	Core accounting services and the delivery of selected financial services and products in a consultative manner.

It's possible to expeditiously move through *Stage 2* and even to skip the stage entirely. In that case, the CPA firm goes directly from providing core accounting and tax services to incorporating selected and coordinated financial services and products in the context of holistic planning. The caveat is that doing so requires a well conceptualized and well executed business plan as well as the proper infrastructure. Such a move can be made however, when the firm is highly motivated at the outset, heavily client-focused, and has a roster of planning-focused accountants with a strong tax orientation.

At this point we need to understand just why the financial advisor is but a stepping stone on the way to becoming a wealth manager.

The Limitations of the Financial Advisor

To understand why becoming a financial advisor is not the same as becoming a wealth manager, we have to take a closer look at what financial advisors do and who they are. A financial advisor is usually described as someone who is *selling* one or more types of financial products – mutual funds, insurance, or estate planning, for instance.

While a workable model, it's limiting for most accountants. Today's financial advisors, as we define them, are not taking into account all of the potential interaction and interplay of the financial products they sell, in particular, how those products can be combined to address a client's complete financial equation over the course of a long and mutually profitable relationship. They're predominantly seeing the client as a one-dimensional figure.

While there's nothing inherently wrong with this approach – it will remain the model for the majority of financial services providers, after all – the CPA firms who never progress beyond this stage are doing a disservice to themselves and, potentially, to their clients. Because accountants have a strong tax perspective as well as broad understanding of both their clients' finances and personalities, merely selling financial products will fall short of providing those clients with the best possible financial solutions. Few other professional advisors have the depth and breath of understanding that high-quality accountants possess. And few are as highly trusted by their clients. By not progressing beyond the financial advisory stage, accountants are minimizing their ability to leverage their deep understanding of the client. By not taking a holistic approach, CPAs will be passing up a substantial and profitable opportunity.

An excellent example of the difference between *Stage 2* and *Stage 3* can be seen in the different way that accountants in either stage would employ private placement variable life insurance, one of the state-of-the-art financial products being used today.

In private placement variable life insurance, advisors help their clients select money managers – often hedge funds – that are wrapped in a life insurance policy. This enables the investments (i.e., the hedge funds) to grow in a tax deferred way. Hedge funds generally generate significant tax bills and the life insurance wrapper helps mitigate (and potentially eliminate) capital gains taxes.

A CPA firm in *Stage 2* providing private placement variable life insurance tends to be focused on the tax benefits of wrapping the hedge funds in the life insurance policy; that is, the firm is focused on the investment aspects of the product and likely to overlook and underutilize its insurance component.

In contrast, a wealth manager could make private placement variable life insurance part of a broader solution. Of course, the direct tax benefits of the product are there, but a wealth manager could also:

- Obtain a substantial tax deduction of more than 75 percent while simultaneously creating a dynasty trust benefiting grandchildren and future generations. This could be done while optimizing the cost/benefit relationship and eliminating the payment of estate and gift taxes.

- Create a conservation trust funded in perpetuity with half the monies coming from matching governmental and other private sources. This solution would create a deferred income stream for the benefit of any heirs that was equal to the net present value of the initial investment.

- Get enhanced investment returns resulting in a doubling of the returns over a 20-year period with private placement variable life insurance (as opposed to not wrapping the investment). In this case, it would be possible to make certain heirs receive all the assets of the estate without paying any income or estate taxes.

- Facilitate a gift of art and the accompanying financial support in perpetuity. This gift would allow the benefactor to generate income for life that will actuarially be two-to-three times larger than the value of the donated gift.

- Create a nonqualified plan for portfolio managers and fund it with their "own" investment performance.

- Create a trust benefiting the grandchildren that can circumvent the need to pay estate taxes on assets of $100 million or more. In this case, the investments provide for lifetime income of $10 million or more with minimal tax obligations.

- Diversify a concentrated and highly appreciated equity position without paying capital gains taxes while concurrently hedging a well diversified portfolio and generating a steady stream of tax-free revenue, all at a net-zero cost.

- Protect investment assets from creditors and litigants while multiplying the investment return and payout (which is also protected even though the client has limited input into the advisory process).

The financial advisor is a transitional role for many CPA firms. However, we fully recognize that a meaningful number of accountants who enter the financial services business will never evolve beyond this role because wealth management isn't in accord with the way they run their business, the wishes of their clientele, or their skill sets and knowledge base. Nevertheless, becoming a financial advisor will enable many accountants to dramatically increase their revenue while better serving their clients.

We believe that the new paradigm for CPA firms is that of wealth management. On one level, this is a holistic and consultative approach to solving a client's financial problems. The answer is not insurance or investments. Instead, the answer is the best advice complemented with the right financial products; that's what wealth management is all about. Wealth management complements the expertise and the way accountants work with their clients. Importantly, it also results in improved client relationships, more profitability from each client, and increased client referrals.

Defining Wealth Management

Let's consider the wealth management model in greater detail. The way we're defining wealth management is somewhat different from the way it's defined by some of the players in the financial services industry. That is, if you were to examine the literature, talk to CPAs who consider themselves or their firms to be wealth managers, or ask financial planners what wealth management is, you'd get a number of different – and sometimes conflicting – answers.

In sum, there are many ways for an accountant to be a wealth manager and a variety of different wealth management platforms to choose from. So which one should a CPA firm opt for?

We believe that the following definition reflects the paradigm-shifting nature that is wealth management:

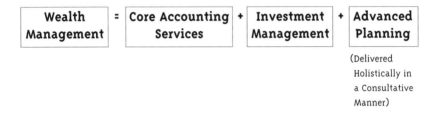

Wealth Management	=	**Core Accounting Services**	+	**Investment Management**	+	**Advanced Planning**

(Delivered Holistically in a Consultative Manner)

Wealth management is really both a platform and a way of working with clients. It's validated by the ability to cross-sell a number of different but interrelated sets of services to a single client. After considering the risk-adjusted returns, the integration opportunity, and the relationship enhancement opportunities, we found that the optimal management platform for accountants is their current core services coupled with investment management and advanced planning.

The Components of Wealth Management

When considering the components of wealth management, we begin with the core accounting services offered during *Stage 1*. For many accountants this includes tax advice and related planning services.

Investment management entails providing investment solutions for clients. This encompasses both transactions and ongoing fee-based business. With respect to transactions, we're talking about basic brokerage (i.e., the buying and selling of securities), managed investments such as "A" class mutual funds, and derivatives such as prepaid forwards. Fee-based business is where the wealth manager receives an ongoing fee to oversee the portfolio. The most common examples of this are mutual fund wrap programs and managed account programs.

Meanwhile advanced planning is composed of one or more of the following four interrelated services:

- **Wealth Enhancement** involves determining the current timing, character, and amount of taxable income, which is usually investment income. In effect, the goal is to manage what taxes are paid and when. There are a wide variety of strategies that can be utilized to enhance wealth, including cashless collars, contingent swaps, prepaid forwards, and charitable remainder trusts.

- **Wealth Transfer** includes basic estate planning employing such strategies as credit-shelter trusts and traditional life insurance. For those clients with a more complicated financial picture and goals, there are a number of more sophisticated approaches to wealth transfer, including self-canceling installment notes and remainder purchase marital trusts.

- **Asset Protection Planning** is a subset of risk management. The aim is to protect the client's wealth against potential creditors and litigants, children-in-law, and potential ex-spouses. The strategies vary widely based on the situation and may include transformation and monetization.

- **Charitable Gifting** is for the philanthropically oriented client. There are many strategies, tactics, and products that a wealth manager can bring to bear on behalf of an affluent client, including private foundations, donor-advised funds, charitable remainder trusts, and charitable lead trusts.

There is a powerful interrelationship between investment management and advanced planning. This is especially the case as the latter often results in "liquifying" tangible assets that subsequently require professional management.

Now let's take a step back and see why these sets of services constitute the optimal wealth management platform for CPA firms.

The Optimal Wealth Management Platform

The optimal wealth management platform was derived empirically. That is, we analyzed the business models of CPA firms and determined that the coordinated combination of investment management and advanced planning results in a cost-effective, client-benefiting platform when placed "on top" of an accountant's core competencies.

The sets of services that are most often considered accretive to core accounting services are:

- **Advanced Planning**, consisting of wealth enhancement, wealth transfer, asset protection, and charitable gifting.

- **Credit**, including mortgages, personal loans, and commercial loans for business owners.

- **Property and Casualty Insurance**, encompassing the entire array of offerings from art and collectibles to liability and yachts.

- **Investment Management**, including providing investment portfolios and a wide range of investment products for clients.

The next question is which of these sets of services should be added to an accountant's core offerings to create the "best" wealth management platform. To make this determination, the analysis we conducted was predicated on three variables: (1) the financial risk-adjusted returns, (2) ease of integration, and (3) the relationship enhancement opportunity. The methodology we employed was based principally on data from other types of advisors who have adopted the wealth management model. Further, we took the fundamental findings and developed a model predicated on extensive research conducted with the empirically derived working patterns of CPA firms.

With respect to each of these variables, a rating of 1.00 is defined as optimal. However, this is "conceptual optimal." In reality, it's just about impossible to achieve a 1.00 rating. What's most important is to see how the various types of services compare to one another.

In Exhibit 2.2, we see that advanced planning is by far the best choice when considering financial risk-adjusted returns. What's critical to understand is the enormous profit that can be generated by advanced planning with affluent clients. Next is investment management and a major factor in the financial risk-adjusted returns of investment management is the retainer-like arrangement with respect to fee-based money management.

EXHIBIT 2.2: **Financial Risk-Adjusted Returns**

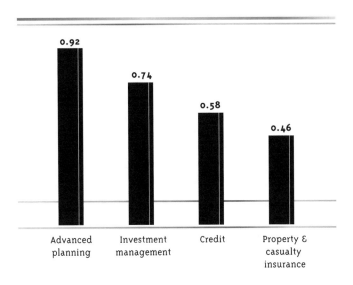

SOURCE: PRINCE & ASSOCIATES, 2002.

When it comes to ease of integration, credit takes top honors (Exhibit 2.3). When clients want credit, it's very easy to bring in the credit specialist who can provide the client with a loan. Next comes investment management, in large part because of the strong preference of CPA firms to rely on turnkey asset management programs (i.e., mutual fund wraps and management account programs). On a comparative basis, advanced planning comes in last due to its intricacies.

EXHIBIT 2.3: **Ease of Integration**

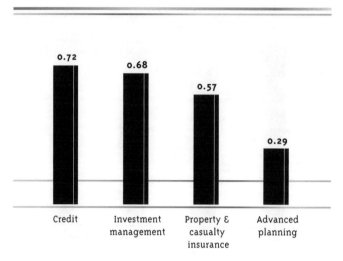

SOURCE: PRINCE & ASSOCIATES, 2002.

The relationship enhancement opportunity is the final variable we'll consider (Exhibit 2.4). In this case, advanced planning is far and away the best way of enhancing a relationship with a client. The reason for this is that advanced planning delves into areas that aren't often addressed by accountants. Specifically, the profiling of the client in advanced planning provides the broadest and most in-depth understanding of the client for all of the services being considered. Also, the problem-solving orientation of advanced planning translates into much deeper relationships with clients. Next in line is investment management which – presuming investment performance is in line with expectations – results in a strong professional relationship with the client.

EXHIBIT 2.4: **The Relationship Enhancement Opportunity**

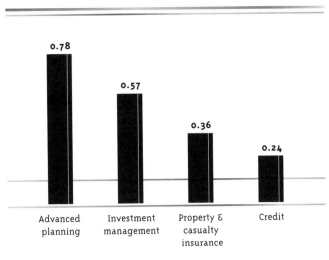

SOURCE: PRINCE & ASSOCIATES, 2002.

In sum, when integrating and evaluating these factors, we find that the best wealth management platform for CPA firms incorporates advanced planning and investment management.

Wealth Management Compensation Arrangements

There are four compensation arrangements used by professionals who have adopted the wealth management model. Across the various types of advisors, we find that most wealth managers rely on a mix of the four. Some arrangements, such as commissions, have been historically associated with certain products like insurance or securities. Other pairings such as asset-based fees tied to insurance are still evolving.

The four primary compensation arrangements are:

- **Advisory Fees:** Sometimes hourly based, sometimes project based, advisory fees range from a few thousand dollars to six figures, and they're commonly charged for core accounting services as well as feasibility studies and other analyses, case design, and implementation. Advisory fees fit quite well with the way many accountants are currently being compensated.

- **Commissions:** For the sale of products such as traditional life insurance or brokerage services as well as derivatives, the wealth manager receives a commission (which can sometimes be negotiated).

- **Asset-based Fees:** The most pervasive form of asset-based fee is fee-based money management such as a managed account. However, there are numerous opportunities when meeting the needs and wants of the wealthy where life insurance can be provided on an asset-based fee arrangement.

- **Performance Fees:** The greatest compensation is possible from performance fees when the accountant/wealth manager's compensation is based on the success of the strategy employed. These fees are calculated as a percentage against a predetermined benchmark within a select time frame.

Strategic Considerations

In this chapter, we've discussed the evolution of accountants to wealth managers. Of course, different firms are at different stages in this evolution because of such factors as the nature of their clientele, the competition, their business model, and the firm's relative success and growth. Regardless of where a firm happens to be, it's a useful exercise to reflect how far the firm's peer group has evolved (Exhibit 2.5). The firm's partners should take the ten accounting firms they know best and consider where they stand with respect to this paradigm shift. Are all of them maintaining the traditional, baseline paradigm of pure accounting services? Or have some of them begun a shift to a new way of approaching their business and their clients? How many have already started to offer financial services (investments and/or life insurance)? Have any become full-fledged wealth managers?

EXHIBIT 2.5: **Auditing a Firm's Competitive Context**

Stage	Definition	Of 10 competing accounting firms, the number that are in each stage
STAGE 1	Baseline paradigm: accountants offer basic accounting and tax services.	
STAGE 2	Transition stage: accountants begin to include the selling of financial products.	
STAGE 3	New paradigm: accountants provide the full range of financial products and services in a wealth management model.	

It's also worth assessing a firm's current revenue model. Most accounting firms that are in *Stage 1* are deriving their revenue entirely from advisory fees. As firms progress through the stages on their way to the wealth management model, we find that they add additional sources of revenue. Exhibit 2.6 will help CPA firms assess their current revenue sources and reflect on the implications of broadening their revenue sources.

EXHIBIT 2.6: Auditing a Firm's Revenue Model

Wealth management compensation arrangements	Percent of revenue from each type	Comments and reflections
Advisory fees		
Commissions		
Asset-based fees		
Performance fees		

Stage 2

THE ACCOUNTANT AS FINANCIAL ADVISOR

CHAPTER 3

Providing Financial Services

"Change your thoughts and you change your world."

NORMAN VINCENT PEALE

Executive Summary

Our research showed us that nearly one out of every five CPA firms had already reached *Stage 2* and nearly half of the remaining firms expected to be offering financial products and services in the next three years.

There's a lot of talk in the accounting world about accountants providing financial services. Accountants are wondering whether they should provide other services in addition to accounting and, if so, how. They're raising many issues about their business models and regularly reevaluating their strategic decisions.

This debate isn't surprising given the profitability and potential of the wealth management model. In this chapter, we'll see who's making the shift and why. We'll also explore the types of strategic thinking CPA firms engage in and the various benefits and consequences. All these points will be backed by statistics and information derived from some of the largest and most thorough studies of strategy in the accounting profession that have ever been conducted. Finally, we'll introduce a tool that will let accountants audit the current strategies of their own firm as well as the business implications of those strategies.

The Decision to Be a Financial Advisor

In *Stage 2* of the paradigm shift, accountants add the sale of financial products to their core CPA services to become financial advisors, and we'll now consider the extent to which accountants have already become financial advisors as well as the extent to which they plan to enter the financial advisory business.

As noted in the previous chapter in our discussion of wealth management, we've found that a major difficulty in analyzing issues methodically is that people will use the same term to mean different things. To reiterate, when we talk about accountants as financial advisors we're talking about accountants who sell financial services. And by financial services we mean life insurance products as well as investment products including transactions compensated by commissions (such as the buying and selling of securities) and fee-based money management.

According to our survey of 1,685 accounting firms, 82.6 percent did not sell investment services to their clients, focusing instead on their core competency, accounting services, and staying at *Stage 1*. Less than one in five had already made the move to *Stage 2* by adding investment services to their offerings.

However, the paradigm shift will pick up momentum over the next few years (Exhibit 3.1), during which time half of all accounting firms said they planned to begin offering investment services. In other words, most firms will have made the move to *Stage 2* by 2005, and many other firms will soon have to decide whether or not they're ready and able to keep up with the competition.

EXHIBIT 3.1: **Accountants Providing Investment Services**

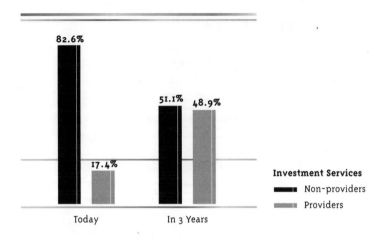

N = 1,685 ACCOUNTANTS.
SOURCE: CEG WORLDWIDE/PRINCE & ASSOCIATES, 2002.

Probing further, we also found that when it came to financial services there was a stronger preference among CPA firms to provide investment products as opposed to life insurance. To offer comprehensive financial services, however, it's best to offer both because they can be very complementary from the client's standpoint.

As was the case with investment services, most CPA firms didn't offer life insurance, yet more than half of those firms that expected to do so by 2005 (Exhibit 3.2). In fact, we believe that many of those firms will have made – or begun to make – the further transition to *Stage 3* by that time.

EXHIBIT 3.2: **Accountants Providing Life Insurance Services**

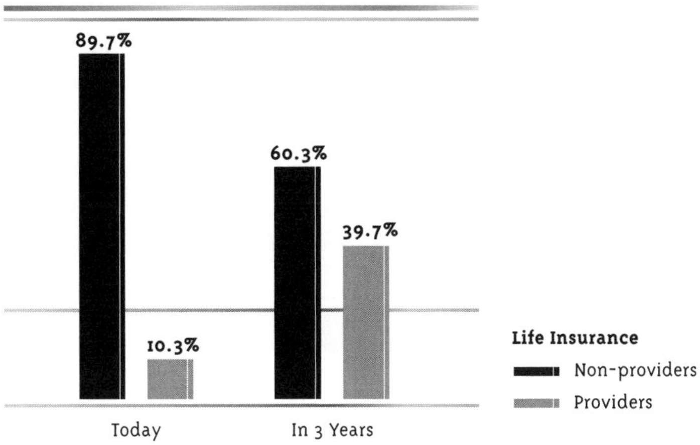

89.7%

60.3%

39.7%

10.3%

Today   In 3 Years

Life Insurance
▬▬■ Non-providers
▬▬▬■ Providers

N = 1,685 ACCOUNTANTS.
SOURCE: CEG WORLDWIDE/PRINCE & ASSOCIATES, 2002.

Strategic Rationale

The CPA firms we surveyed had clear rationales for their actions and intentions that may help other firms and individual accountants crystallize their thoughts about their practice and where they want to take them.

You'll recall that some accountants said they didn't expect to be offering financial services in three years. They cited a number of reasons as the basis for their decision (Exhibit 3.3), with most feeling that entering the financial services field represented an insurmountable conflict of interest. The fact that they were dedicated to financial and tax analysis and reporting would help them, they believe, maintain their objectivity, a particularly compelling issue in the wake of the Andersen/Enron debacle. More than four out of five did not want to make the move because they saw themselves as accounting professionals, not insurance or investment specialists. Finally, more than three-quarters did not want to compromise their standing as the trusted advisor to their clients.

EXHIBIT 3.3: **Reasons For Not Being a Financial Advisor**

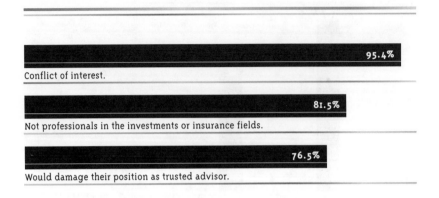

N = 861 ACCOUNTANTS WHO SAY THEY WILL NOT OFFER FINANCIAL SERVICES IN THREE YEARS.
SOURCE: CEG WORLDWIDE/PRINCE & ASSOCIATES, 2002.

The top rationale cited by those firms that said they would make the shift and offer financial services in the next three years was the belief that they would better serve their clients (Exhibit 3.4). Other firms cited the fact that the accounting profession is changing and they have no choice but to move with it if they want to increase their revenues, keep up with the competition, grow their businesses, and hold on to their clients (let alone get new clients).

EXHIBIT 3.4: **Reasons for Being a Financial Advisor**

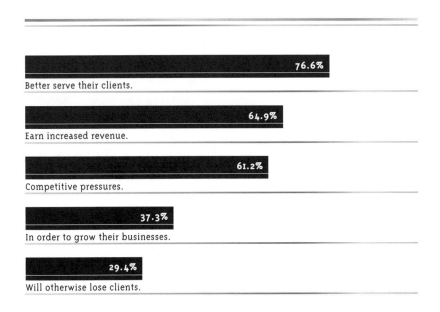

Better serve their clients. — 76.6%

Earn increased revenue. — 64.9%

Competitive pressures. — 61.2%

In order to grow their businesses. — 37.3%

Will otherwise lose clients. — 29.4%

N = 824 ACCOUNTANTS WHO ARE OR INTEND TO BE FINANCIAL ADVISORS.
SOURCE: CEG WORLDWIDE/PRINCE & ASSOCIATES, 2002.

The Bias Against Life Insurance

While many CPA firms already felt the effects of the paradigm shift toward financial services and were ready to change, our research confirmed that there was a lingering bias against life insurance. We undertook a study to further explore the thinking behind this preference in detail, surveying 112 accountants who already offered investment products but not life insurance.

There were many reasons that accountants were hesitant to add life insurance to round out their financial services offerings (Exhibit 3.5). The greatest obstacle was that CPAs were concerned that commissions communicated a lack of objectivity or bias. Commissions on the sale of insurance products also connoted a real or perceived lack of independence on their part, a reservation that persisted in spite of the commissions or fees that some of those surveyed received for selling investment products to their clients.

Quite a few felt that insurance agents were less respected than accountants and they were concerned that their clients might view them as insurance agents. About half were uncomfortable with the compensation, perhaps because they didn't fully understand all of the costs involved in developing and implementing insurance products. Others said they were too unfamiliar with insurance carriers and insurance products to be active. Finally, many CPA firms and insurance agents were in strategic alliances whereby they exchanged referrals and some of the accountants were worried that offering life insurance would jeopardize the alliances and referrals.

EXHIBIT 3.5: **Reasons Not to Provide Life Insurance**

76.8%
Concerned that commissions communicate bias or a lack of independence.

58.7%
Concerned about clients viewing them as insurance agents.

49.6%
Uncomfortable with the size of the compensation.

38.2%
Unfamiliar with carriers and/or products.

22.6%
Concerned that insurance agent referrals will evaporate.

N = 112 ACCOUNTANTS WHO OFFER INVESTMENT SERVICES BUT NOT LIFE INSURANCE.
SOURCE: CEG WORLDWIDE/PRINCE & ASSOCIATES, 2001.

As we'll see later in this book, many of these reasons for not offering life insurance are untenable in the current competitive environment. Life insurance is an essential solution to many complex financial problems of the affluent. In fact, the reason for the paradigm shift is that accounting, life insurance, investment, tax, and all the other related services are best for clients if they're offered as an integrated package. The lingering bias against life insurance is unsound and can actually work against both the accountants who do not offer it and the clients of those accountants who do not get the chance to buy life insurance.

Strategic Considerations

With the paradigm shift in full swing, CPA firms and individual accountants will have to make strategic decisions. What will their strategy be in response to the changes that are underway? Will they offer financial services? Will they make a distinction between investment services and life insurance?

From a strategic perspective, certain costs and benefits are associated with each decision (Exhibit 3.6). For example, firms that choose a strategy of innovation and aspire to be the first to respond to changes in their industry are *Pioneers*. Pioneering firms have the benefit of what are called "first-mover" advantages. That is, they're seen as industry pacesetters and leading thinkers. Such firms also interest clients who are equally innovative in their thinking and are therefore attracted by the firm's bold approach.

Of course, not all firms embrace change. Some firms sit on the sidelines and wait to see the outcome of change before taking it on themselves. This is called the *Fast Follower* strategy. The benefits of this wait-and-see strategy include the fact that there's less time and money devoted to tracking the industry. The risk of making a major mistake is also lower because the benchmarks have been established by someone else. The trade-off is the abdication of first-mover status and all that that entails.

Some firms never change unless they absolutely have to. Such firms only make a change after half or more of all the other firms in their industry have done so. The strategy of these firms is to lag. By being a *Laggard* in strategic terms, they realize the lowest costs of all and their risk profile is minimal. But such a strategy can be costly because the *Laggards* cannot differentiate their services in order to create value for their clients, and the only clients left over are those in niche markets; the mainstream (and most profitable) clients will gravitate to the *Pioneers* and *Fast Followers*.

EXHIBIT 3.6: Costs and Benefits of Strategic Actions

Strategic Approach	Benefits	Costs
Pioneers	First mover advantages, attract innovative clients, preempt competitors.	Learning curve.
Fast Followers	Lower costs, benchmarks available.	Loss of first-mover status.
Laggards	Lowest costs, can find niches.	Lack of differentiation.

When industries are in flux and undergoing a paradigm shift, these strategies are implemented in real time – they happen quickly and firms have to respond accordingly. This is the situation right now for accountants entering, or considering entering, the financial services arena. The CPA firms that have already started to offer financial services are *Pioneers*. Those who will start to do so between now and the end of 2005 are *Fast Followers*. Firms that haven't responded to the paradigm shift by 2005 are *Laggards* and they risk becoming noncompetitive.

EXHIBIT 3.7: **Auditing a Firm's Strategy**

Year the firm has (or will offer) investment services.	
Factors favoring the move into investment services.	
Factors against the move into investment services.	
The firm's strategic investment services position.	[ ] *Pioneer* [ ] *Fast Follower* [ ] *Laggard*
Year the firm has (or will offer) life insurance.	
Factors favoring the move into life insurance services.	
Factors against the move into life insurance services.	
The firm's strategic life insurance position.	[ ] *Pioneer* [ ] *Fast Follower* [ ] *Laggard*

Exhibit 3.7 has been created to help accountants assess the strategy of their firm and its competitors. By using it, a CPA can decide whether his or her firm's strategic approach is active or passive. It's the nature of paradigm shifts to occur whether people want them to or not. They have a life of their own. The only choice we can make in the midst of a paradigm shift is to align ourselves with it to some degree, and the more we know about our own capabilities, the better suited we will be to not only withstand but profit and thrive from such a shift.

CHAPTER 4

The Financial Services Opportunities for Accountants

"There is nothing like returning to a place that remains unchanged to find the ways in which you yourself have altered."

NELSON MANDELA

Executive Summary

Individuals and small business owners who already obtain financial services from accountants are very satisfied with both the quality of the products and the level of service they receive. There's also considerable interest in financial services among clients who don't currently get them from their accountants.

Paradigm shifts occur because competitive and market forces align to produce change. For the shift to occur, both the market forces and competitive trends need to be complementary, that is, moving in the same direction. If one or the other is not moving, or if they are in opposition, there will not be a paradigm shift.

In the last chapter, we looked at the paradigm shift from the perspective of CPA firms. Now we'll look at the other side of the equation, their clients, to see what they're thinking and doing and whether they're resisting or embracing the changes in the accounting industry. We'll consider whether individuals and businesses are receptive to directly compensating accountants for financial products and services. Finally, in light of that information, we'll demonstrate why we believe accountants can be more successful as financial advisors and, ultimately, as wealth managers.

Evaluating the Opportunity

As usual, in order to answer these questions, we evaluated the issue empirically by surveying the clients of CPA firms. One group was comprised of 1,521 individuals who had an annual income of $75,000 or more, and the second group was made up of 719 small business owners who had been in business 10 years or more and whose business generated at least $10 million annually. Each small business had 500 or fewer employees.

In each case, less than one in ten of the clients and small businesses was getting financial products from their accountants (Exhibit 4.1). Just as we saw earlier when we discovered that accountants could be thought of as *Pioneers*, *Fast Followers*, or *Laggards*, so, too, can clients. The clients who already turn to their accountants for financial services are themselves *Pioneers*. Not all clients are ready to adopt this new paradigm, but there was some evidence of clients having moved to *Stage 2*.

EXHIBIT 4.1: **Currently Obtaining Financial Products From Accountants**

9.1% 8.8%

Individuals   Small business
owners

N = 2,241. SOURCE: PRINCE & ASSOCIATES, 2000.

Of course, this finding is a function of the limited number of accountants who currently provide financial products. As we saw in **Chapter 3: Providing Financial Services**, not many clients have had the option of obtaining financial products from their accountants. In fact, of the 2,241 firms we surveyed, only 17.4 percent offered investment services and just 10.3 percent offered insurance services. So it follows that few clients would have even had the chance to obtain such products and services from their current accountants.

The critical question then was not how many of the clients surveyed had turned to their accountants for financial products, but how satisfied they were. Having made the leap in faith that their accountants could deliver a broader range of services, were they pleased with what they got? The answer was a resounding yes. Among the individuals and small business owners who obtained financial products from accountants, better than four out of five were "highly satisfied" with both the quality of the products and the level of service they were receiving (Exhibit 4.2).

EXHIBIT 4.2: Level of Client Satisfaction with the Financial Services They Obtain From Accountants

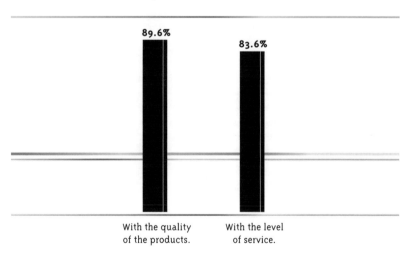

89.6%
83.6%

With the quality
of the products.

With the level
of service.

N = 201 INDIVIDUALS AND BUSINESS OWNERS WHO TURN TO ACCOUNTANTS FOR
FINANCIAL PRODUCTS. SOURCE: PRINCE & ASSOCIATES, 2000.

The level of client satisfaction is an extremely important – if not the most important – metric in service businesses. In many different service industries, not just financial services, satisfaction has been shown to correlate highly with customer and client repurchase. In the services industry, it takes a great deal of "investment" to obtain a single new client. That's why it's so critical to retain clients and, as one might expect, satisfaction is the single greatest predictor of client retention. Satisfaction is an even better predictor than the technical aspects of the service provided. Satisfaction is also highly correlated with client referrals. It's much more cost-efficient to obtain new clients through referrals than it is through prospecting.

In this analysis, satisfaction is a useful metric for us because of the extent to which it predicts client behavior. Two behavioral measures of satisfaction are whether those clients would obtain additional financial products from the same provider and whether they would provide referrals. On both these metrics, accountants who already offered financial products scored well (Exhibit 4.3). Nearly all of the clients said they would turn to their accountants for more financial products and better than four out of five said they would refer people they knew.

Note that these results are high compared to findings in other industries, which may reflect on the quality and integrity of the accounting profession and the overall trust that clients place in their accountants.

EXHIBIT 4.3: **Likely Future Actions of Clients Getting Financial Products From Accountants**

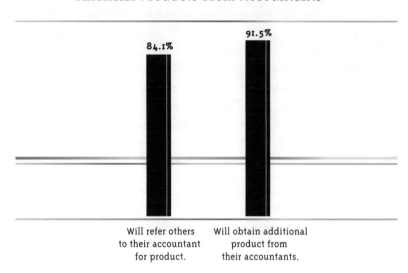

N = 201 INDIVIDUALS AND BUSINESS OWNERS WHO TURN TO ACCOUNTANTS FOR
FINANCIAL PRODUCTS. SOURCE: PRINCE & ASSOCIATES, 2000.

In conclusion, our research showed that a small but not insignificant number of clients were already getting financial services from their accountants. They were highly satisfied and, importantly, they said they would look to those accountants for other financial services and also provide referrals. This is hard evidence of the existence of – and value in – the paradigm shift in the accounting industry today. Indeed, if these relationships continue to grow and expand, accountants will become formidable competitors for other advisors on a number of financial services fronts.

The Opportunities With Prospects

As the next step, we wanted to find out whether clients who had not yet turned to accountants for financial services (prospects) might do so and, again, a majority said they would.

Overall, about half of the 2,039 prospects said they would be "very interested" in obtaining investment products from their accountant (Exhibit 4.4) and nearly three-quarters said they were "very interested" in getting insurance products from their accountants.

But does that interest translate into the intention to actually purchase? In this case, there's evidence that it does. Looking only at the affluent prospects who had not obtained products from an accountant, we found that just over half of them said they would be "very likely" to obtain investment products from their accountants. More than two-thirds said they would be "very likely" to get life insurance products from their accountant. Among small business owner prospects, almost half were "very willing" to obtain retirement plans (including the accompanying investment options) from their accountants, and better than four out of five said they were "very willing" to get insurance services from their accountants.

The high level of interest in insurance products was especially revealing in light of the bias against insurance among accountants that we've already noted. Given the interest of the prospects we surveyed – and the fact that it eclipses their interest in investment services – accounting professionals may wish to rethink their attitudes about offering life insurance.

The reason for the strong interest in life insurance is the interconnectedness of life insurance and tax issues. From deferred compensation to estate planning, taxes are a driving force in addressing client problems, and life insurance can provide solutions to many tax issues. In turn, tax issues are a recognized area of expertise for accountants.

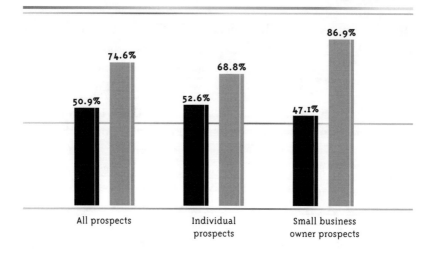

EXHIBIT 4.4: **Percent of Prospects "Very Likely" to Obtain Financial Products From Their Accountant**

■■■■ Investment products
■■■■ Insurance products

All prospects: 50.9% / 74.6%
Individual prospects: 52.6% / 68.8%
Small business owner prospects: 47.1% / 86.9%

N = 2,039 PROSPECTS. SOURCE: PRINCE & ASSOCIATES, 2000.

Why Prospects Will Not Obtain Financial Products From Their Accountants

As the next step, we wanted to find out why some prospects said they wouldn't turn to accountants for financial products (Exhibit 4.5). The top three reasons were:

- The financial products were not presently needed.

- The accountant or accounting firm did not possess the necessary expertise.

- There was a perceived conflict of interest if accountants provided financial products.

The most common reason the prospects gave for not wanting financial products from accountants, that they didn't see a need, didn't mean that the prospects weren't interested in investment products per se, but that they didn't see any reason for getting those products from their accountants. The respondents already had one or more professionals providing them with investment products and didn't see the need for another.

The next significant reason was that the prospects were worried that accountants didn't possess the requisite expertise. These clients believed that accountants should stick to what they knew and not expand into financial services without first assuring clients of their new skill-sets.

Prospective clients were far less worried about any potential conflicts of interest. Overall, they didn't think a conflict of interest would be a barrier to using an accountant for investment services. This was true for individual prospects as well as business owners, and it's of interest given the degree to which accountants were concerned about potential conflicts of interest and how their clients might see them in that regard (see page 38).

EXHIBIT 4.5: **Reasons Not to Obtain Investment Services From Accountants**

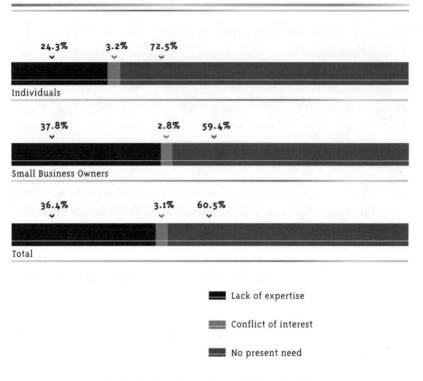

24.3%   3.2%   72.5%

Individuals

37.8%   2.8%   59.4%

Small Business Owners

36.4%   3.1%   60.5%

Total

■ Lack of expertise

■ Conflict of interest

■ No present need

N = 1,002 PROSPECTS. SOURCE: PRINCE & ASSOCIATES, 2000.

Though our research told us that prospects were more likely to look to their accountants for insurance products than investment products, we also pursued the reasons that they would not do so (Exhibit 4.6). The reservations proved to be similar. Again, the number one reason prospective clients didn't obtain insurance services from accountants was that they hadn't felt the need to do so.

A substantial proportion of the prospects thought their accountants lacked the expertise to be in the insurance business. Whether the accountants in question were or were not competent when it came to insurance was not the issue. The point was that a significant proportion of individuals and small business owners perceived that to be the case. Finally, while potential conflicts of interest were a major concern among accountants, the prospects were far from concerned.

EXHIBIT 4.6: **Reasons Not to Obtain Insurance Services From Accountants**

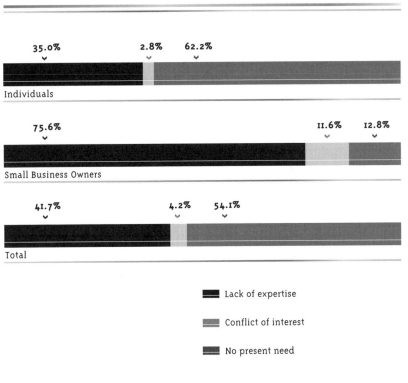

35.0%   2.8%   62.2%

Individuals

75.6%   11.6%   12.8%

Small Business Owners

41.7%   4.2%   54.1%

Total

■ Lack of expertise

■ Conflict of interest

■ No present need

N = 1,002 PROSPECTS. SOURCE: PRINCE & ASSOCIATES, 2000.

In the case of both investment and insurance products, as we've seen, the prospects said that the main reason they weren't getting those services from accountants was a lack of necessity – they were already getting them from other advisors. This brings us back to the limitation of *Stage 2* in the paradigm shift. To successfully sell products and services in *Stage 2*, a client must want those services from accountants, and they may not because they may already be getting them from other sources. In *Stage 3*, however, they're persuaded to get those products and services because a wealth manager can demonstrate how those services fit into a total financial solution. As the one who delineates that solution, the wealth manger is also the one best positioned to provide the component parts. When *Stage 3* is reached, we've found that many clients who had no prior interest in turning to their CPA firms for financial products and services will begin to do so.

The lesser doubts about expertise, we believe, can be effectively addressed by client education and awareness – by demonstrating to clients that the CPA firm has a well-thought-out and full-fledged financial capability. Since most firms will be outsourcing financial services, they can also bring in those resources to meet with the clients and demonstrate their expertise.

No "Andersenitis"

Unfortunately, there's a whole new set of issues and image problems affecting the accounting industry thanks to the Arthur Andersen/ Enron situation.

Some accountants are worried that there will be significant fallout from the Andersen/Enron situation and that everyone in the accounting industry will be tainted, regardless of their reputation and record. For many, the message is the opposite of the one we've been counseling – accountants should not venture beyond traditional accounting to dabble in financial services or consulting lest they get in over their heads.

In order to explore the extent to which the clients of smaller accounting firms have residual concerns about their relationships in the wake of Andersen/Enron, we did another study. Since one of the most controversial elements of the Andersen/Enron relationship revolves around the appropriateness of the financial services support that Andersen provided, we focused on that in particular.

We developed a sample of 171 clients who relied on their accountants for tax preparation and investment advisory services. Each client had to have at least $100,000 in investable assets and be broadly aware of the Andersen/Enron situation.

We asked these clients how Andersen/Enron would impact their accounting relationships and the response was an unequivocal vote of confidence (Exhibit 4.7). Nearly three out of four said they were "very likely" or "certain" that they would add additional financial assets for the accountant to manage. Not only that, almost two-thirds said they planned to refer other people to their accountant for investment services. Only a handful said they were going to move assets away from the accountant to another investment professional, and the few that were making such moves did so for reasons that had nothing to do with Andersen/Enron.

EXHIBIT 4.7: Intended Actions

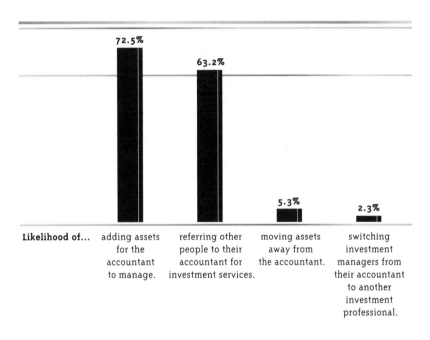

Likelihood of...	adding assets for the accountant to manage.	referring other people to their accountant for investment services.	moving assets away from the accountant.	switching investment managers from their accountant to another investment professional.
	72.5%	63.2%	5.3%	2.3%

N = 171 INVESTORS. SOURCE: PRINCE & ASSOCIATES, 2002.

To verify these conclusions, we conducted a second study among 266 investors who didn't have any of their assets managed by their accountants. We wanted to know how they felt about accountants in general and whether or not they would look to their accountants for financial products and services in the future (Exhibit 4.8). Again, the responses were positive, with more than half of the respondents saying they would entrust their accountants with their assets if those accountants offered financial products and services. Nearly half said that if their accountant provided such services they would in turn provide referrals. Clearly, these results reflect well on the high level of trust and confidence that accountants have earned from their clients.

EXHIBIT 4.8: **Accountant Opportunities**

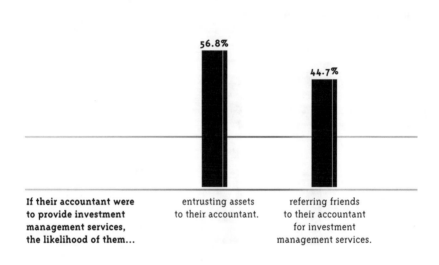

	56.8%	44.7%
If their accountant were to provide investment management services, the likelihood of them...	entrusting assets to their accountant.	referring friends to their accountant for investment management services.

N = 266 INVESTORS. SOURCE: PRINCE & ASSOCIATES, 2002.

Strategic Considerations:
The Voice of the Client

When assessing or revising an accounting firm's strategy, it's essential to include input from the firm's current clientele. The data described in this chapter was collected from affluent clients across the United States, but each firm's clients will have a wide range of different needs, desires, and interests that have to be considered.

In almost every service businesses, we've found that the top 20 percent of clients account for 80 percent of revenues and profits, and we suggest that those are the clients that should be approached. In Exhibit 4.9, we've provided a systematic way for accountants and accounting firms to conduct this analysis. First, they should list their top clients, both individuals and business owners. Then those clients should be approached, one at a time, and canvassed about any change in strategic direction that's being contemplated. This can be done during one of the regularly scheduled meetings with these clients.

In this instance, clients should be approached as counselors. It should be explained to them that there's an ongoing dialogue about the future of the accounting industry and of changing client needs. The clients should be told that some firms are beginning to move in the wealth management direction and that the firm in question is considering such a move. Finally, they should be asked what they think the pros and cons are of such a move. In order to not upset their clients, accountants will need to deftly manage the conversation.

During the discussion, particular attention should be paid to client concerns about some of the issues that we've already identified; an absence of need, a lack of expertise, or conflict of interest. Such issues and concerns should be noted, not addressed. The clients can then be asked whether or not they might turn to their accounting firm for investment services and insurance products if those concerns could be allayed.

Finally, any findings should be compared to the data reported in this chapter. Are clients likely to be receptive to a firm moving in the direction of offering financial services? Are they open to thinking about the firm as a resource for investment management and insurance solutions? Above all, are they ready to accept the new paradigm?

EXHIBIT 4.9: **Auditing a Firm's Strategy**

List top 10 *individual* clients	Rate need for or interest in investment management	Rate need for or interest in insurance services

List top 10 *business owner* clients	Rate need for or interest in investment management	Rate need for or interest in insurance services

CHAPTER 5

Critical Success Factors in Financial Services

"Decide what you want, decide what you are willing to exchange for it. Establish your priorities and go to work."

H. L. HUNT

Executive Summary

The top three critical success factors cited by those CPA firms that have successfully entered the financial services field are: 1) having partners identify prospects for the financial services practice, 2) creating strategic alliances with experts in life insurance and investments, and 3) being able to access financial services professionals on a case-by-case basis. Firms that have entered but then exited the financial services business offered three main reasons for their failure: 1) the firm was never fully committed to the business, 2) implementation was problematic because there was not a change "champion" among the partners, and 3) there were conflicts with the firm's financial services provider(s).

Those CPA firms that are trying to decide whether, and when, to enter the financial services field, have their pioneering colleagues to look to. Those leading CPA firms have already created business models that work. This means that the successful models and benchmarks — the critical success factors — of the pioneering firms are available for study and emulation.

For all of the first-mover advantages, not every firm can be a *Pioneer*. And for *Fast Followers*, there's a great deal to be gained by reviewing the trial and error process of these business trailblazers. To further illustrate *Stage 2* and *Stage 3* of the paradigm shift, we'll now take a close look at research based on those CPA firms that were among the first to make the move toward the wealth management model.

What It Takes to Build a Successful Financial Advisor Practice

Many factors enter into creating a successful transition from a traditional accounting firm to a CPA firm that also offers financial products (Exhibit 5.1). According to the CPA firms that have made the transition to *Stage 2*, however, the top three factors relate to resources and support structures. And, as we shall see, getting these three critical success factors right is essential for any firm that wants to make the move from *Stage 1* to *Stage 2*.

The single most critical success factor is having partners who are able to identify prospects for the firm's evolving financial services practice. CPA firms are by-and-large positioned to sell financial services to their current accounting clients, but in the long term they will need an ongoing stream of new financial services prospects to make the model work. The best way to do this is to build that pipeline.

Not surprisingly, then, the second most critical factor is the importance of creating strategic alliances with experts in the life insurance and investments business that will be part of that pipeline. Right now, most accounting firms prefer to bring in financial expertise on an as-needed basis. That is, once they've qualified a client and understood the client's need, they summon an investment or insurance expert to do the work. The accountant will be the primary relationship manager and be responsible for integrating all of the services performed for the client. At this point in time, relatively few accounting firms are restructuring in order to bring on board their own investment advisors and insurance producers, and only a handful are joining multidisciplinary wealth management firms. As the paradigm shift continues, however, bringing those experts on board may well become the norm.

Given the current reliance on outsourced resources, it follows that the third most often cited critical success factor was the ability to access financial services professionals on a case-by-case basis. When expertise is sourced from outside, it's naturally harder to control than when the skills are within the firm. Because the cost of bringing the expertise inside is prohibitive for all but the largest CPA firms, most end up sourcing investment and insurance expertise from outside. Managing it on a dynamic basis is an ongoing challenge.

Practice Management

Practice management issues were next on the list of critical success factors. The best advice from firms that had made the transition to *Stage 2* was to get the CPA firm's infrastructure right. Specifically, CPA firms that have successfully added financial products said it was crucial to get their firm properly aligned around their expanded offerings.

More than two-thirds of those firms stressed the importance of developing a detailed business plan for their financial services practice. The ability to carefully delineate implementation actions, cost them out, and project profitability were critical to success. Such a business plan can be used to compare internal and external benchmarks and to reach outsourcing and investment decisions. By adroitly using this information, the CPA firm can – over time – best utilize its resources.

Accountants experienced in this transition say that it's equally important to put in place a well-designed compensation system that promotes the cross-selling of financial products. If the firm wants its accountants to approach their clients and offer them financial products, there must be an incentive to do so. Further, if the firm wants those accountants to bring in and manage financial services professionals, the accountants will have to be directly compensated for doing so. In our experience, there are no hard and fast rules for designing the compensation model save for there being a direct correlation between providing a client with financial services and being paid appropriately.

Getting into new lines of business is not free, of course. Two-thirds of the firms that have moved to *Stage 2* said that careful planning was vital to ensuring that the resources committed to the financial services practice were wisely used. Many accountants had made errors as they sought to become financial advisors. In some cases, in fact, they had abandoned the attempt to move to *Stage 2* (Exhibit 5.2) because of the high costs.

It's also essential that any new strategy is understood – and committed to – by all partners. If all of the partners aren't on board, the new venture may very well fail. Whether the route taken to build consensus is partner off-sites, other meetings, or daily interaction, it's critical to continue to reinforce the logic – and potential profitability – of being in the financial services business.

Partners also need to know what their options are. In our view, those options are 1) to do nothing, 2) to make changes very slowly (the *Laggard* alternative), 3) to make those changes fairly quickly (the *Fast Follower* approach), or 4) be a *Pioneer*. Before making any strategic move, however, it's essential that everyone involved can articulate the options and also have enough time to explore the pros and cons of each option.

The next step is to discuss and illuminate the criteria that should be used to make a choice. Are individuals and the partnership trying to optimize firm growth, personal income, productivity, or some other value? What are the goals and aspirations of the firm and its leadership? The answers to these questions can be especially illuminating and also lead to a decision, ideally one that involves anything but stagnation. Assuming a decision is made, the next step will be implementation.

More than half of our respondents stressed the importance of developing a detailed marketing plan for the financial services practice, and nearly as many cited the importance of having the right infrastructure and support staff in place. Other factors cited included refining the way the financial services practice operates, asking clients for the new life insurance or investment business, and putting one partner in charge of the financial services practice.

EXHIBIT 5.1: **What It Takes to Build a Successful Financial Services Practice**

89.4%
Having partners identify prospects for the financial services practice.

74.8%
Creating strategic alliances with experts in life insurance and/or investments.

70.5%
Being able to access financial services professionals on a case-by-case basis.

69.8%
Developing a detailed business plan for the financial services practice.

67.2%
Having a compensation system that promotes the cross-selling of financial services.

67.0%
Committing the resources to the financial services practice.

63.8%
Having all partners committed to the financial services strategy.

54.0%
Developing a detailed marketing plan for the financial services practice.

44.9%
Having the infrastructure and support staff in place to do the business.

44.1%
Refining the way the financial services practice operates.

38.8%
Asking clients for the new life insurance or investment business.

28.6%
Having one partner in charge of the financial services practice.

N = 824 ACCOUNTANTS PROVIDING FINANCIAL SERVICES. SOURCE: CEG WORLDWIDE/PRINCE & ASSOCIATES, 2002.

For *Fast Followers* in particular, understanding the benchmarks of the *Pioneers* in the field is a big help. *Fast Followers* can reduce their risk level by emulating the successes of the pioneering firms. They can take advantage of the successes and avoid the pitfalls. Just looking at the successful firms, however, is not enough. They must also learn from the experiences of those firms whose experiment with financial services failed.

Financial Advisors No More

As might be imagined, it's exceedingly difficult to get precise information regarding the number of accounting firms that have entered and then exited the financial services business. We believe there are relatively few such firms because the rewards of a well-planned transition are usually substantial. However, we were able to locate enough firms that have advanced to and then retreated from *Stage 2* to empirically evaluate the issue.

First, we wanted to know why these firms had gotten out of the financial services business and, for the most part, the reasons related to implementation and practice management issues (Exhibit 5.2). The top reason these accounting firms decided to exit the financial services field was compelling: because their firm had not fully committed to the financial services business to begin with. Everyone wanted to have done it, but no one wanted to do it. Because of a less than complete commitment, the firms never brought on board the expertise they needed to be able to competently serve their clientele. These findings reinforce the necessity of building a strategic consensus among all of an accounting firm's partners before moving to *Stage 2*.

Another outcome of this less than wholehearted commitment was poor implementation. More than two-thirds, for example, confessed that they took the easy way out and never moved beyond the "low hanging fruit" of current clients. In other words, they never tried to move beyond the clients who themselves had requested financial services. Surprisingly, more than half of the firms had never even asked their clients if they were interested in financial services. The failure may have had to do with the fact that partners were not – as they saw it – fairly compensated for providing financial services to clients.

There were also some underlying conflicts with the way the firms aligned with their financial services provider(s). To the chagrin of a number of accountants, some of the insurance agents and investment managers proved to be bad fits with the way they did business either because they were overaggressive or because they seemed not to be sufficiently client-centric.

As we saw in **Chapter 2, An Evolution: From Accountants to Wealth Managers**, a major concern of those CPA firms that have not yet ventured into financial services was that they might lose accounting referral sources. They were afraid of what might happen if they suddenly begin to compete against a firm that used to send referrals their way. Based on this sampling, however, that is not an issue, as less than one in ten of the firms said they left the financial services field because they had jeopardized their referral pipeline.

EXHIBIT 5.2: **Reasons for Leaving the Financial Services Business**

85.9%	
The firm never fully committed to the business.	
71.0%	
The firm did not have the requisite expertise.	
67.2%	
The firm never moved beyond the "low hanging fruit."	
58.6%	
Clients were not asked for their financial services business.	
49.1%	
Partners were not fairly compensated for providing clients.	
33.4%	
There was a conflict with the way the financial services provider(s) did business.	
9.6%	
The firm lost accounting referral sources.	

N = 149 ACCOUNTANTS WHO LEFT THE BUSINESS.
SOURCE: PRINCE & ASSOCIATES, 2002.

So far, the guideposts for moving to *Stage 2* are clear. Pioneering CPA firms have established good business and practice benchmarks for other firms to follow. The few CPA firms that have tried and then left financial services report that they retreated because of poor implementation or a failure to line up the right strategic partners. In sum, good planning and implementation are crucial to any such transition.

Perpetually Getting Ready

Careful, reasoned, and thoughtful planning and implementation are essential for any accounting firm interested in moving from *Stage 1* to *Stage 2*. That's why we say that another major determinant of success is actually taking action. Quite a few accountants have spent years preparing to enter the financial services business but have yet to do so. A survey of 104 accountants who said they were about to become financial advisors resulted in some interesting findings that will help other CPA firms plan their own implementation or transition.

Good homework takes time, and these firms reported that they had invested the time to do it right (Exhibit 5.3). In fact, all of them had spent at least a year planning. Half said they had been planning to add financial services for from one-to-three years and better than one-third had been working at it for three-to-five years. One in ten had been looking at the opportunity for more than five years. The "right" amount of planning time will clearly vary from firm to firm. Certainly, at the beginning, when uncertainty is greatest, it's wise to proceed cautiously. As markets mature, however, we would expect the planning cycle to be shorter.

EXHIBIT 5.3: Getting Ready to Enter the Financial Services Business

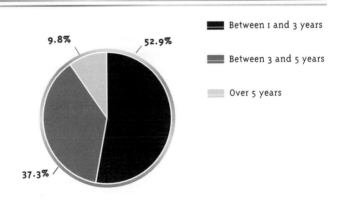

N = 102 ACCOUNTANTS. SOURCE: PRINCE & ASSOCIATES, 2002.

So how have these accountants been spending their time? More than two-thirds of them said they were preoccupied with learning how all of the financial products worked (Exhibit 5.4). Interestingly, they were far less concerned with becoming adept at the various types of planning, a skill that's more associated with the transition to *Stage 3*.

Another oft-cited reason for delay was getting the right human resources in place. More than half of the firms said that no one in the firm has taken "ownership" of the financial services practice. As we've seen, without an advocate for financial services, there's little chance of the initiative getting off the ground. Making sure all the accountants in the firm are completely and unreservedly on board is also a common concern, as it should be. Finally, nearly half said that it takes time to find the right financial partners to team up with.

EXHIBIT 5.4: What's Holding Them Back?

67.6%	Learning how all the products work.
57.8%	No one in the firm has taken "ownership" of the financial services practice.
48.0%	Finding the best financial advisor to team up with.
42.2%	Making sure all the accountants in the firm are on board.
18.6%	Becoming adept at the various types of planning.

N = 102 ACCOUNTANTS. SOURCE: PRINCE & ASSOCIATES, 2002.

Strategic Considerations

The following checklist of critical success factors (Exhibit 5.5) was designed to help accounting firms moving to *Stage 2* assess the risk and keep track of their progress in making the transition.

EXHIBIT 5.5: **Checklist of Critical Success Factors**

READINESS FACTOR	RATE YOUR PROGRESS ON EACH ITEM		
Having partners identify prospects for the financial services practice.	[ ] to do	[ ] working on it	[ ] complete
Creating strategic alliances with experts in the life insurance and investments industries.	[ ] to do	[ ] working on it	[ ] complete
Being able to access financial services professionals on a case-by-case basis.	[ ] to do	[ ] working on it	[ ] complete
Developing a detailed business plan for the financial services practice.	[ ] to do	[ ] working on it	[ ] complete
Having a compensation system that promotes the cross-selling of financial services.	[ ] to do	[ ] working on it	[ ] complete
Committing the resources to the financial services practice.	[ ] to do	[ ] working on it	[ ] complete
Having all partners committed to the financial services strategy.	[ ] to do	[ ] working on it	[ ] complete
Developing a detailed marketing plan for the financial services practice.	[ ] to do	[ ] working on it	[ ] complete
Having the infrastructure and support staff in place.	[ ] to do	[ ] working on it	[ ] complete
Refining the way the financial services practice operates.	[ ] to do	[ ] working on it	[ ] complete
Asking clients for life insurance or investment business.	[ ] to do	[ ] working on it	[ ] complete
Having one partner in charge of the financial services practice.	[ ] to do	[ ] working on it	[ ] complete

Stage 3

THE ACCOUNTANT AS WEALTH MANAGER

CHAPTER 6

The Wealth Management Advantage

*"We all have big changes in our lives that
are more or less a second chance."*

HARRISON FORD

Executive Summary

The wealth management platform combines disciplines — traditional accounting, investment management, and advanced planning — and delivers them in a highly consultative manner. Though few accounting firms have evolved to this stage, adopting the wealth management model has been demonstrated to increase revenues and profitability in the private banking, life insurance, and brokerage industries.

As a result of the paradigm shift in the accounting industry, *Stage 3* is the evolutionary model for CPA firms moving into the financial services industry. Wealth management, a holistic consultative approach to working with clients, is nothing less than the future. This does not mean that an accounting firm cannot thrive if it only progresses to *Stage 2*. But, to truly leverage the very nature of the client relationship created with quality professional accounting services, the answer is wealth management.

This section of the book is devoted to a comprehensive overview of the wealth management platform for accountants. Wealth management is the end point of the current paradigm shift and understanding what it means is critical for those accountants who expect to be providing financial services over the coming decade.

As we shall see, there are many ways for an accountant to become a wealth manager. Because they understand risk-adjusted returns, integration opportunities, and relationship enhancement opportunities, a wealth manager can be a person who combines traditional accounting functions with investment management and advanced planning.

In the scheme of things, however, relatively few CPA firms have effectively embraced the wealth management model. That stands in marked contrast to *Stage 2* which many CPA firms have reached (or are at least moving toward), thus providing us with ample data to work with. There are clear indications that most accountants want to move to the highest level of client servicing, which is only logical as it best uses the inherent advantages of the accountant to improve client relationships and increase profitability. However, because of some of the difficulties associated with establishing and maintaining a wealth management practice, there are not many accountants who have successfully made the move to *Stage 3*. As a result, when it comes to accountants as wealth managers we have a great deal of anecdotal evidence but not enough hard data to educe statistically valid conclusions.

We do know that some accountants are becoming wealth managers because we regularly hear of situations where an accountant has engaged in a holistic problem-solving approach that integrates the use of various financial products and services. The result has been highly satisfied clients and higher profitability per client. At the same time, we've been involved in assisting CPA firms become wealth managers and our first-hand experience fully validates the benefits of *Stage 3* for CPA firms and their clients.

Despite the lack of data for accountants reaching *Stage 3*, there's plenty of available data on other financial advisors who've become wealth managers, and we can look to them for lessons that are applicable to accountancy.

We've conducted research on the viability of the wealth management model with private bankers, insurance agents, and with brokers. With each of these financial advisors, we looked at the barriers to and benefits of becoming a wealth manager, compensation and resource issues, and critical success factors for their practice development. In addition, we assessed the value of the wealth management model for each of these types of advisors. These studies of the different types of financial advisors illustrate the various benefits of the wealth management model (Exhibit 6.1). Specifically, our study of private bankers illustrated revenue enhancement, our study of insurance agents income enhancement, and our study of brokers production enhancement.

EXHIBIT 6.1: Benefits of the Wealth Management Model

Benefit of the Wealth Management Model	Case Study
More revenue for accountants	The study of private bankers
More income for accountants	The study of insurance agents
More production for accountants	The study of brokers

Accountants can weigh the benefits of wealth management by looking at how other professionals approach the field and serve clients. Indeed, by considering the research findings in greater detail, we will clearly see the benefit of the wealth management model for accountants.

Private Banking and Wealth Management

Private bankers have traditionally been the gatekeepers for banking, credit, trust, and investment services for affluent clients. It's a position that is increasingly under siege from all other financial advisors – including accountants.

Overall, not that many private banks are providing the entire wealth management platform. Although they're offering a number of different types of services, advanced planning is usually not in the mix. The myriad reasons for not committing to wealth management will already be familiar to readers of this book. Nevertheless, there are some private banks that have implemented a comprehensive wealth management model.

We wanted to know how these private banking wealth management models had fared. Had wealth management proven to be a more successful model? What were the challenges and benefits of evolving to wealth management? Finally, what could accountants learn from this experience?

In order to look at the viability of the wealth management model within private banking, we conducted a study of 98 private banks. In these private banks, the minimum account size was $500,000 in liquid assets. All of the banks were engaged in some form of wealth management. We found that there were three discernable types of wealth management platforms:

- **Basic:** The private banks provided investment management and trust services as well as classic banking services such as transaction accounts. This is analogous to *Stage 1* of our paradigm shift model.

- **Enhanced:** These private banks provided the basic package and added credit to their offerings. For the banking industry, this corresponds to *Stage 2* of our paradigm shift model.

- **Comprehensive:** This is where the private bank offered a comprehensive set of financial offerings as well as advanced planning, matching *Stage 3* of our paradigm shift model.

Of the 98 private banks, 46 offered the basic wealth management model, 29 the enhanced wealth management model, and the remaining 23 the comprehensive wealth management model (Exhibit 6.2). Note that these findings show that one in four private banks have already moved into wealth management as we have defined it.

EXHIBIT 6.2: **The Wealth Management Models of Private Banks**

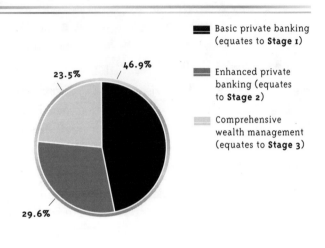

Basic private banking (equates to **Stage 1**)

Enhanced private banking (equates to **Stage 2**)

Comprehensive wealth management (equates to **Stage 3**)

N = 98 PRIVATE BANKS.
SOURCE: PRINCE & ASSOCIATES, 2002.

Using the profitability figures from these banks, we were able to build a mathematical formula that allowed us to compare the three wealth management models. That is, we statistically adjusted for a number of variables such as the wealth of the clientele and length of time they were patrons of the private bank. This methodology enabled us to compare the private banks in an apples-to-apples manner.

In order to illustrate the profit variances, we created an index. To create the index, we set the base profitability of the private bank with the *Basic* version at $1,000 [Exhibit 6.3]. Private banks that have implemented the *Enhanced* version of wealth management earned significantly more, or $1,134 on the index. Finally, private banks offering *Comprehensive* wealth management had better than twice the profitability of those using the *Basic* platform.

EXHIBIT 6.3: **Profitability Comparison of the Private Bank Wealth Management Platforms**

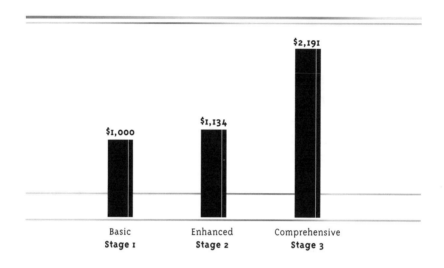

| Basic | Enhanced | Comprehensive |
| Stage 1 | Stage 2 | Stage 3 |

N = 98 PRIVATE BANKS.
SOURCE: PRINCE & ASSOCIATES, 2002.

What can we conclude from this data? First, private banks are already moving into wealth management and, if accountants are to effectively compete for affluent clients, they will have to compete on this same high level – *Stage 3*. Secondly, in the world of private banking, the ability to offer a broader wealth platform results in greater profitability. Moreover, the addition of advanced planning proves exceptionally profitable in the private banking context. Given those results, we can expect more and more private banks to evolve to a comprehensive wealth management platform.

Life Insurance and Wealth Management

In order to sell life insurance, life insurance agents frequently provide planning services. Because life insurance is a solution to many estate planning needs, it's often sold in the context of estate planning services. As a result, the life insurance industry has long done planning; what it has not done until recently is investment management, banking, and personal or small business financial management (accounting). In order to best assess the results of wealth management in the insurance industry, we surveyed life insurance agents who provided wealth transfer planning.

The sample entailed two matched sets of life insurance agents who made between $75,000 and $100,000 a year selling life insurance. Over two years, a total of 266 insurance agents (133 in each group) were followed. The two groups were matched statistically so that we could compare apples-to-apples.

One group (*Life Only*) continued to market life insurance and provided wealth transfer planning services. This is the group that provides traditional insurance services and is analogous to *Stage 1* and *Stage 2* of the paradigm shift model.

The second group (*Life + Investments*) also sold life insurance, provided wealth transfer services, and incorporated fee-based assets management services in the form of a mutual fund wrap or managed account. This is *Stage 3*, comprehensive wealth management, for insurance providers, and the members of the group that added fee-based investment management saw their income surpass that of the group that continued to sell only life insurance (Exhibit 6.4).

EXHIBIT 6.4: **Comparing Incomes**

$139,000

❮ $101,000 in life insurance commissions and $38,000 in fee-based investment income

$87,000

| Life Only | Life + Investments |
| Stage 1 & Stage 2 | Stage 3 |

N = 266 INSURANCE AGENTS. SOURCE: PRINCE & ASSOCIATES, 2002.

Over the two-year time frame, the average annual income for the *Life Only* group was $87,000 with all of the income coming from commissions on the sale of life insurance. For the *Life + Investments* group, the average annual income over the same time period was $139,000. The majority of the income – $101,000 – came from commissions on life insurance, but $38,000 came from fee-based investment management.

In sum, those life insurance agents that had adopted a wealth management approach were able to significantly increase their income. Fee-based investment management alone resulted in a 16.1 percent increase in life commissions. The reason for this was straightforward; it's often easier to get a prospect's interest in fee-based investment management than in wealth transfer. However, once that prospect becomes a client, the life insurance agent who has established rapport can identify the client's need for life insurance.

Another advantage for the *Life + Investments* group was the fact that its life insurance agents were positioned to generate more annuity-type revenues. That is, they were set to collect investment advisory fees on an ongoing basis without necessarily having to make another sale. As was the case with private bankers, we can conclude that when insurance agents adopted a wealth management model, their profitability and income went up significantly.

Brokers and Wealth Management

While every broker's practice is in some way unique, they do cluster into three broad categories based on the extent to which they have adopted the new paradigm. For the purposes of comparison and explanation, we are matching the broker business model categories to the three stages of the paradigm shift. However, due the nature of the brokerage industry, the parallels are not that precise. These three broad categories are:

- **Product Specialists:** Focused on a product niche and products that are all investment centered. A broker who specializes in managed accounts or 144 stock or fixed income is an example of a product specialist. This kind of broker would be at *Stage 1* in the paradigm shift.

- **Investment Generalists:** Provides (or potentially provides) a wide range of investments, and does not have a more comprehensive financial planning orientation. This kind of broker corresponds to *Stage 2* of the paradigm shift.

- **Wealth Managers:** A comprehensive or holistic approach to working with clients that takes into account both sides of the client's personal P&L statement. This broker has a planning orientation that's validated by cross-selling services. This is *Stage 3* of the paradigm shift.

In our study of 4,106 brokers, *Product Specialists* accounted for 912 of the total and *Investment Generalists* for nearly two-thirds, 2,689. There were only 505 brokers who could be classified as *Wealth Managers* (Exhibit 6.5).

EXHIBIT 6.5: The Business Models of Brokers

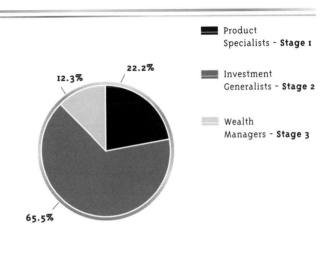

N = 4,106 BROKERS.

SOURCE: THE WORLD OF REGISTERED REPRESENTATIVES

[WWW.IIHIGHNETWORTH.COM], 2002.

With the fall of the dot.coms and the subsequent recession, the brokerage business has not been healthy of late. Over the course of 2000-2001, per broker production dropped 34.9 percent on an annualized basis. However unfortunate that has been for clients, it does offer an excellent laboratory for seeing which business model has fared best during the downturn.

Of the three broker business models, the wealth management model was far and away the most profitable over this period (Exhibit 6.6). In fact, it is the only business model to generate a positive delta. On average, each *Wealth Manager* actually improved production by 9.3 percent at a time when overall production dropped 34.9 percent. Brokers adopting the wealth management model have been able to outperform *Product Specialists* and *Investment Generalists* by capitalizing on the built-in attributes of the business model, including leveraging client relationships, cross-selling, and providing products and services not tied to the markets. Once again, the wealth management model was the most profitable.

EXHIBIT 6.6: **Production Changes by Business Model**

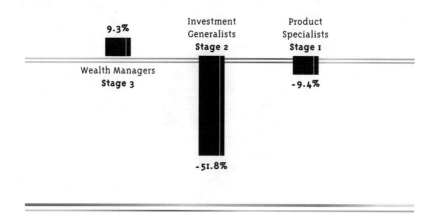

N = 4,106 BROKERS. SOURCE: THE WORLD OF REGISTERED REPRESENTATIVES
(WWW.IIHIGHNETWORTH.COM), 2002.

The results were even more compelling when we only looked at the 391 brokers who dealt with affluent clients (Exhibit 6.7). In this case, the *Investment Generalists* again provided the lowest returns (-51.1%) while the production of the *Product Specialists* actually rose slightly. The *Wealth Managers*, however, increased their production by an impressive 36.9 percent.

EXHIBIT 6.7: **Production Changes for High-Net-Worth Brokers**

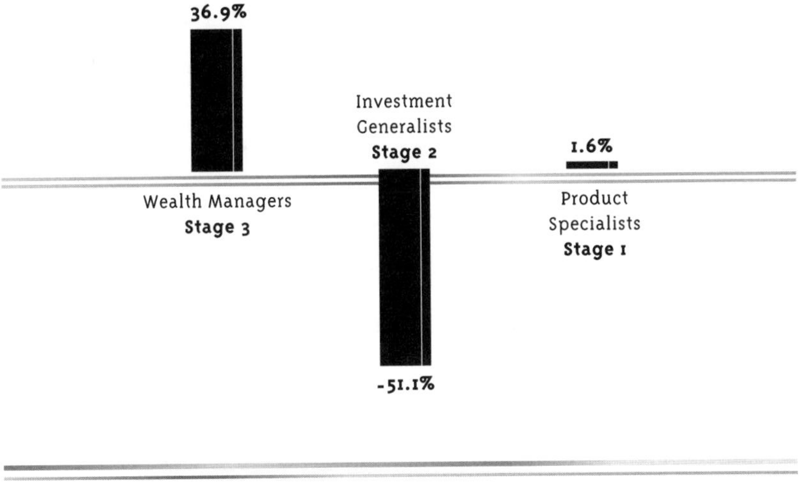

36.9%

Investment
Generalists
Stage 2

1.6%

Wealth Managers
Stage 3

Product
Specialists
Stage 1

-51.1%

N = 391 BROKERS. SOURCE: THE WORLD OF REGISTERED REPRESENTATIVES
(WWW.IIHIGHNETWORTH.COM), 2002.

Strategic Considerations

All of the above data reinforces our thesis that, aside from providing better client solutions, the greatest benefit of pursuing a wealth management business model will be financial rewards for the accounting firm. Whether the provider is a private bank, an insurance agent, or a broker, the result of moving into wealth management is the same: financial success.

This data can also be used to analyze the financial needs of an accounting firm from a top-down basis (we will do a bottoms-up or client-centered projection at the end of the next chapter). Each firm can use the worksheet below (Exhibit 6.5) to choose the appropriate financial factors, note where the firm is today, select a future planning horizon (three or five years is common), and decide on a target.

EXHIBIT 6.8: **Auditing a Firm's Strategy**

FINANCIAL FACTOR	CURRENT SITUATION ON SELECTED FACTOR(S)	GOAL (IN__YEARS)
Firm revenue		
Revenue per partner		
Partner income		
Profitability per client		
Productivity		

This exercise will enable individual accountants and accounting firms to look at any gap that may exist between where they are now and where they want to be at the end of the planning period. Accounting practices (whether measured by revenue, income, or profitability) are not growing as they might. If growth is the goal, the wealth management model needs to be examined now.

CHAPTER 7

Building the Wealth Management Platform

"The universe is change; our life is what our thoughts make it."

MARCUS AURELIUS

Executive Summary

The specific steps to building the wealth manager platform are: 1) conduct an internal assessment (including a critical evaluation of the client base), 2) evaluate and select one of the four business model alternatives (*Build, Buy, Joint Venture, or Referrals*), 3) build the wealth management infrastructure, and 4) establish an expert support structure.

Throughout this book, we've been making the case for transitioning those CPA firms that are interested in becoming players in the financial services business to the wealth management model. As we've seen, some CPA firms have already made this evolutionary step and others are in the process of doing so. Based on their experience, as well as the insights of other types of financial advisors who have embraced the wealth management model, we were able to benchmark successful transitions and document the pitfalls.

In this chapter, we'll walk through the step-by-step process that will allow CPA firms to successfully make the transition to *Stage 3*. The specific steps to becoming a wealth manager are:

1. Conduct an internal assessment.

2. Evaluate the four business model alternatives.

3. Build the wealth management infrastructure.

4. Establish an expert support structure.

Conduct an Internal Assessment

By an internal assessment, we mean a thoughtful and thorough process whereby a firm develops a deep understanding of its strengths, weaknesses, opportunities, and any impediments to its success as a wealth manager. It's best to do an internal assessment with the full partnership involved, if possible. In our experience, the most successful transitions to wealth management have leveraged all the resources and support of the firm's partnership. If everyone's in agreement regarding the firm's strategic vision, implementation is comparatively straightforward.

In the course of its assessment, a firm may discover that it's not ready or well suited to make the move to *Stage 3*. Indeed, the first task of an internal assessment is to check on the readiness and commitment of the firm to be in the financial services business. At that point, the critical questions are:

- Should the firm be in the financial services business?

- Do the partners want to be wealth managers?

- What is the optimal way to deliver wealth management?

If the decision is made to not enter the financial services business, the firm stays at *Stage 1*. If it decides to be in the financial services business, the firm needs to determine if it makes more sense to be a financial advisor or a wealth manager. If the firm has already reached *Stage 2*, it then has to decide if it's prepared to advance to *Stage 3*. Assuming that the firm makes the decision to go to *Stage 3*, it then has to choose a wealth management business model.

Going back to the beginning of the internal assessment, a firm can reach consensus by taking a critical look at its client base because the wisdom and success of the move to *Stage 3* will often hinge on the ability of that client base to support the initiative.

In analyzing a firm's current clientele, it's best to focus on the top 20 percent of high-net-worth and corporate clients. As noted earlier, most firms get 80 percent of their revenues and profits from 20 percent of their clients. Further, it's essential to think of these clients in terms of their prospective financial services needs and not solely in terms of the revenues they already generate (Exhibit 7.1). More often than not, current clients will sustain a firm during its transition to *Stage 3*. In fact, those clients may provide enough business that it could be years before a firm has to look for new clients.

EXHIBIT 7.1: **Criteria for Evaluating Existing Clientele**

A firm should develop segmentation schemes based on in-house data for its clients:

- **Net-worth**
- **Investable assets**
- **Income**
- **Occupation**
- **Complexity of financial situation**
- **Comfort with risk**
- **Density of personal and professional network**

The internal assessment should also include a look at the CPA firm itself as well as its employees (Exhibit 7.2). That assessment should comprise an analysis of the skill sets resident in the firm and any gaps that may exist. Start with technical expertise. To move to *Stage 3*, a firm will very likely have to find a way to bring new skills into the practice or find a way to source them outside in a reliable way. The critical skill sets are investment management and advanced planning. Later in this chapter we'll review the different ways of accessing these capabilities. Right now, the task is to see whether or not (and to what extent) people already in the firm can bring those talents to the table.

Marketing skills are equally important. The goal (and metric) of a successful transition to wealth manager is practice growth, and that means bringing on new clients, providing more products and services, or both. In any case, marketing capabilities are essential, particularly the abilities to create a pipeline of prospects and to manage client relationships for long-term retention. In addition, a firm will want to be certain that it has the operational abilities necessary to manage a wealth management practice.

EXHIBIT 7.2: **Criteria for Evaluating Firm Skill Sets**

- **Technical expertise**
  Investment management
  Advanced planning
- **Marketing capabilities**
  Prospecting
  Relationship management
- **Operational abilities**
  Managing a financial services practice

With data on clients and on the firm's practice in hand, it's possible to develop alternative scenarios for transitioning a practice (Exhibit 7.3). The first thing to consider is the nature of the transition – how much of a change is desired – which entails a "gap analysis." A gap analysis starts with a view of where the practice is today in terms of revenues and profits and where it wants to be. The size of this gap will determine the degree of change that has to be made.

The next step is to plan specific practice changes as regards any new products and services that will be brought on. For example, a firm may want to start with investment products, then expand into insurance, and finally offer the gamut of wealth management services, representing a rapid evolution from *Stage 1* to *Stage 3*. The point is that a profit and loss statement as well as a cash flow forecast can be created for each in order to develop scenarios for filling the gap. At the same time, the firm can detail the resources that will be required and any obstacles that come to mind to generate more accurate cost analyses. Clearly, the more detailed these analyses are, and the more developed the thinking, the more accurate each transition scenario will be. With several scenarios to consider, the firm will be ready to select a high-potential scenario.

EXHIBIT 7.3: **Criteria for Scenario Planning**

- **Gap analysis**
- **Identify opportunities**

  Revenue projections

  Anticipated obstacles
- **Cost structure**

  Profitability calculations
- **Select the high-potential scenario**

Evaluate the Four Business Model Alternatives

Conceptually, there are four basic business models that a CPA firm can adopt to deliver wealth management services to its clients (Exhibit 7.4). Note that the business models are not exclusive. That is, a CPA firm can employ more than one business model at a time. Also keep in mind that the business models are conceptual. That means, operationally, there is a certain amount of overlap.

EXHIBIT 7.4: **Business Model Alternatives**

BUILD	The CPA firm creates its own financial services expertise from scratch.
BUY	The CPA firm buys a financial advisory firm or hires financial advisors.
JOINT VENTURE	The CPA firm enters into a formal equity or revenue sharing joint venture with a financial services firm.
REFERRALS	On a case-by-case basis, the CPA firm refers its clients to financial advisors for predetermined compensation.

When considering which business models are appropriate, there are a number of variables to weigh (Exhibit 7.5). Factors affecting which, if any, business models a firm elects to adopt include the cost of implementation and time to market. A firm should also take into account how well each option aligns with its culture, values, and way of doing business. Finally, the firm should take into consideration any initial and ongoing training requirements.

EXHIBIT 7.5: Key Considerations in Business Model Selection

	BUILD	BUY	JOINT VENTURE	REFERRALS
Cost to implement	**High:** must train staff.	**High:** successful firms require a premium.	**Medium:** some up-front investment is required.	**Low:** can leverage existing relationships.
Time to market	**Long:** extensive licensing requirements.	**Long:** M&A effort intensive and extensive.	**Medium:** initial deal needs to be struck, also follow-up.	**Short:** may already have basis.
Cultural re-alignment requirements	**Very High:** nature of work very different.	**Very High:** different nature of work and personalities.	**Moderate:** need to learn other's style.	**Easiest:** arms-length relationships.
Initial training requirements	**Very High:** extensive training for licensing.	**Medium:** need for cross-training in order to leverage.	**Medium:** need to join in prospecting and qualification.	**Low:** just enough for good referrals.
Ongoing training requirements	**High:** need to maintain licensing.	**Medium:** for dedicated staff.	**Low:** for maintenance.	**Low:** just enough for good referrals.
Profit/ business potential	**High:** good fit with paradigm shift model.	**High:** good fit with paradigm shift model.	**Moderate to High:** depends on arrangement.	**Low:** least value added by CPA firm.

As the above chart illustrates, each business model has characteristic benefits and costs. Each is viable for a certain type of CPA firm. Some want greater control and are willing to go the *Build* or *Buy* routes. While these two business models are the most capital intensive, have the highest training requirements, and take the longest to implement, they offer the greatest potential return. At the other end of the spectrum, the *Referral* model offers the easiest path to getting into the wealth management business but the lowest profit potential. For many firms, the *Joint Venture* model may represent a viable middle ground between the other options in terms of ramp-up time and future revenues.

Building the Infrastructure

The infrastructure support system typically entails agreements with a number of other types of financial institutions. One of the most important of these is the arrangement an accounting firm establishes with a broker/dealer. The broker/dealer needs to be able to provide the requisite wealth management expertise in the form of an expert support system as well as an array of products and services (including training). The selected broker/dealer should be positioned to leverage its relationships with product vendors (such as investment management and life insurance companies) and to provide not only top-notch products with the greatest possible compensation but educational support as well.

In many ways, the infrastructure issue is comparatively straightforward, but it must be securely in place before any progress can be made. A certain amount of due diligence will reveal the available broker/dealers, their product lines, the value-added services they offer, and compensation arrangements.

Establish and Expert Support Structure

In our discussion, we have defined the optimal wealth management platform as the marriage of investment management and advanced planning with traditional CPA services as the foundation. This wealth management platform is not expensive to install because so much of it can be established on a variable basis. While this mode of entry places the least burden and risk on the CPA firm, it also creates the greatest opportunity.

There are two pivotal elements to any wealth management platform: 1) the expert support structure, and 2) the accompanying infrastructure (see above). The expert support structure is composed of the expertise that accountants can call on when needed. This can be a challenging support network to structure, and it's best done over time with the advice and input of professionals expert in investment management and advanced planning. Some of these experts work for boutique firms while others can be secured through institutional relationships (these relationships are often managed by professionals in the expert support structure).

What the expert support structure should look like for any given firm is a function of the skills, knowledge, and talents of the accountants in the firm and the needs of its clients. This should be revealed by an assessment of the firm and its clientele today as well as a forecast for where the firm and its clients will be once the strategic plan has been implemented. The odds are good that no individual or team that's currently in-house will have the knowledge and skill set to be able to provide uniformly high quality and cutting-edge thinking to the diverse wealthy individuals, families, and businesses in their client base. As a result, the accounting firm and/or its broker/dealer must create the expert support structure.

In order to compete for the referrals and renewal business of affluent and business clients, it's essential to have a support system made up of the top experts in their respective fields. The CPA firm must also make sure that any experts they partner with will provide knowledge and insight in a way that complements the accounting firm's core competencies and business style. Having those experts on board has a number of benefits including a lower level of risk, a higher level of profit potential, and peace of mind for the CPA firm that partners with them.

It must be remembered that these experts will be interacting with the CPA firm's clients, and what they do will reflect on the firm. That's why it's essential to consider three key criteria when selecting investment management and advanced planning specialists for the expert support structure. The first two are straightforward – integrity and professionalism. The experts should also have experience in working with accountants. The professional culture of an accounting firm can be quite different than that the specialists are familiar with and, in order to ensure an effective partnership, the specialists must be able to understand how accountants work and adapt accordingly. In the best relationships, there's a high degree of mutual respect.

Strategic Considerations

At this stage, it's important to begin to systematically create client databases that can be the basis for a client relationship management system. The kinds of information needed to serve an accounting client should be augmented by data needed to serve the same client from a wealth management perspective. Exhibit 7.6 shows the type of data that should be collected at a minimum. Collecting, storing, and updating data can be costly, so the rationale for any additional data collection should be well established in advance. (The client information-gathering process is further detailed in our discussion of the Whole Client Model™ (beginning on page 108).

EXHIBIT 7.6: **Develop Wealth Management Databases**

DATA ELEMENT	SIGNIFICANCE	COMMENTS AND NOTES
Net worth	For advanced planning, especially estate planning.	
Investable assets	For investment management.	
Income	For financial planning.	
Occupation	For individual-business planning.	
Complexity of financial situation	To make the case for integration.	
Risk tolerance	Affects entire planning posture.	
Density of personal and professional network	For referrals and business development.	

In addition to creating and implementing client systems, it's essential to profile the CPA firm's wealth management skill sets. Exhibit 7.7 lists the critical skills accounting firms will want to access on a regular basis. As we've seen, there are many different ways to access these skills, but the first step is clarification as to whether or not they already exist in the firm to any degree. The key skills are investment management, advanced planning, marketing capabilities such as prospecting and relationship management, and the operational ability to manage a financial services practice.

EXHIBIT 7.7: **Wealth Management Skill Set Audit**

	SKILLS RESIDENT WITHIN THE FIRM	PLAN TO SOURCE THOSE CAPABILITIES
Technical expertise: investment management		
Technical expertise: advanced planning		
Marketing capabilities: prospecting		
Marketing capabilities: relationship management		
Operational abilities: the ability to run a wealth management practice		

CHAPTER 8

Critical Success Factors Revisited

"We must become the change we want to see."

MAHATMA GANDHI

Executive Summary

A successful transition to the new wealth management paradigm hinges on paying strict attention to critical success factors, including having one partner in charge, creating the right infrastructure, building alliances with experts in investment management and advanced planning, and ensuring that firm members can readily access that expertise.

At this point, we've made the case for the paradigm shift and shown the number of accounting firms already moving from *Stage 1* to *Stage 2* as well as those considering the move to *Stage 3*. We've also laid out the implementation tasks that need to be accomplished between each of these stages. It only remains for us to review the critical success factors that define success for those CPA firms making the final transformation to a wealth management practice (Exhibit 8.1).

Most of these critical success factors are similar to those integral to the *Stage 1* to *Stage 2* transition. For instance, it's essential that all of a firm's partners are deeply committed to change and, as noted. having one partner in charge will greatly ease the transition. Creating the support infrastructure is also critical. Alliances with experts in investment management and advanced planning need to be forged, and firm members need to be able to access this specialized support as needed. Detailed implementation plans are likewise a must. There needs to be a comprehensive business plan for the overall wealth management practice and its marketing wing. In addition, plans need to be put in place for a compensation system that will promote the cross-selling of the full range of wealth management services. Well-thought-out plans will ensure that the right resources are committed to the transition to wealth management.

EXHIBIT 8.1: **Critical Success Factors**

FOR THE TRANSITION BETWEEN STAGE 1 AND STAGE 2	FOR THE TRANSITION BETWEEN STAGE 2 AND STAGE 3
Have partners identify prospects for the financial services practice.	Have partners identify prospects for the wealth management practice.
Source life insurance and investment products.	Create strategic relationships with specialists in investment management and advanced planning.
Ensure the ability to access financial services professionals on a case-by-case basis.	Ensure ability to access state-of-the-art expertise as needed.
Develop a detailed business plan for the financial services practice.	Develop a detailed business plan for the wealth management practice, including the internal assessment.
Have a compensation system that promotes the cross-selling of financial services.	Have a compensation system that promotes the cross-selling of the full range of services.
Commit the necessary resources to the financial services practice.	Commit the necessary resources to the transition to wealth management and the ongoing practice.
Make sure that all of the partners are committed to the financial services strategy.	Make sure that all of the partners are committed to the wealth management strategy.
Develop a detailed marketing plan for the financial services practice.	Develop a detailed marketing plan for the wealth management practice.
Have the infrastructure and support staff in place.	Have the infrastructure and support staff in place.
Refine the way the financial services practice operates.	Refine the way the wealth management practice operates.
Ask clients for their life insurance or investment business.	Position innovative solutions to a client's financial problems.
Have one partner in charge of the financial services practice.	Have one partner in charge of the wealth management practice.
	Sharpen the focus on the affluent; apply consistent pressure to move upscale.
	Adopt value-based pricing.
	Create the wealth management client pipeline.

While we have already reviewed many of these critical success factors, there are three additional ones that are unique to the *Stage 2* to *Stage 3* transition. They are the need to continually upgrade the practice in terms of the affluence of its client base, the appropriateness of value-based pricing, and the creation of a sustainable wealth management client pipeline. The rest of this chapter is devoted to a detailed examination of these three critical success factors.

Focusing on the Affluent

The greatest opportunities for a wealth management practice are among the affluent and the businesses they control. In study after study conducted year after year, our research has confirmed that – for the most part – the more money people have, the more complex their financial situation becomes. As individuals (and often as business owners) they have a wide range of investment management, estate, tax, and related financial needs, concerns, and issues that have to be addressed. Equally important, as they become wealthier, our research has established that the affluent rely increasingly on professionals to manage their financial affairs. And, because of the level of trust they have in their accountants, the affluent are willing to accept them in their expanded role as wealth managers. This is the essence of our discussion of the paradigm shift and our argument for a comprehensive wealth management platform.

Recognizing the importance of the affluent, it's instructive to get a feel for the size and scope of the high-net-worth market both in the United States and abroad. As one of the most stable and open countries in the world, the United States attracts the monies of the affluent of all other countries. This often takes the form of investments in both public and private companies. It also takes the form of residences owned and used by the affluent. Therefore, from the perspective of wealth management, the wealthy from around the globe have a variety of needs that are impacted by this country's tax laws and related regulations. These global wealthy have a need for U.S. advisors to help them manage an often sizable portion of their wealth.

In order to estimate the size of the affluent market, we should define our terms (Exhibit 8.2). In our research, the *low-end affluent* have a net-worth of $1 million to $5 million and, for the most part, the members of these families often do not consider themselves wealthy. Furthermore, a relatively small proportion of their wealth is liquid. The *affluent* control from $5 million to $25 million in assets. Next comes the *supra-affluent* with a net-worth of $25 million to $150 million, followed by the *mega-affluent* with fortunes ranging from $150 million to $500 million. At the pinnacle of the private wealth pyramid are the *maxi-affluent* who each have in excess of $500 million.

EXHIBIT 8.2: **Defining the Affluent**

LEVEL	WEALTH RANGE
Low-end affluent	$1M to $5M
Affluent	$5M to $25M
Supra-affluent	$25M to $150M
Mega-affluent	$150M to $500M
Maxi-affluent	$500M+

SOURCE: ADVANCED PLANNING WITH THE ULTRA-AFFLUENT [WWW.IIHIGHNETWORTH.COM], 2002.

With the parameters established, the next challenge is to size each of these affluent market segments. Because there's no database that one can turn to, the tools of statistics and extrapolation have to be used to model the market and we have designed such an analytic model to fill this information gap. This model permits us to estimate the number of affluent families as well as the amount of wealth they control. The data was collected from 133 different sources such as think tanks, financial institutions, industry consultants, academicians, and governmental organizations. Our sources included The Global Policy Forum, New York University, The Lazard Trust, FinCEN, and The Soloton Society.

Because of the inherent limitations of analytic models, we calculated a best estimate, a low-end estimate, and a high-end estimate (Exhibit

8.3). Our best estimate is that there are more than 17 million families who are millionaires and, as might be expected, the vast majority are among the low-end affluent.

EXHIBIT 8.3: **Sizing the Affluent Worldwide**

LEVEL	LOW-END ESTIMATE	BEST ESTIMATE	HIGH-END ESTIMATE
Low-end affluent	15,488,000	16,712,000	19,824,000
Affluent	442,680	531,610	645,510
Supra-affluent	49,220	58,990	62,380
Mega-affluent	5,670	7,640	8,691
Maxi-affluent	1,170	1,940	2,580
Total	15,986,740	17,312,180	20,543,161

SOURCE: ADVANCED PLANNING WITH THE ULTRA-AFFLUENT [WWW.IIHIGHNETWORTH.COM], 2002.

In addition to estimating the number of the affluent (the potential client base), we also sought to estimate the wealth that they control. By combining the wealth brackets included in the definition of wealth with the number of people in each segment, we were able to develop total global market scope projections (Exhibit 8.4). As shown, the global wealth controlled by the affluent is projected to be at least $49.4 trillion and could be as high as $90.9 trillion. Importantly, for our purposes, a substantial portion of that global wealth is concentrated in the United States, and another substantial portion is invested here.

EXHIBIT 8.4: **Scoping the Affluent Worldwide**[1]

LEVEL	LOW-END ESTIMATE	BEST ESTIMATE	HIGH-END ESTIMATE
All affluent	$49.4 trillion	$69.5 trillion	$90.9 trillion

SOURCE: ADVANCED PLANNING WITH THE ULTRA-AFFLUENT [WWW.IIHIGHNETWORTH.COM], 2002.

[1] It's important to note that in all of our estimates of assets controlled by the affluent we capped the wealth of the maxi-affluent at $1.2 billion for methodological reasons, though there are clearly many among the ranks of the maxi-affluent who exceeded the cap.

Adopting Value-Based Pricing

Accountants customarily charge fees for the services that they provide. Advisory fees are also very important in the wealth management model. This would seem to make for an easy transition for accountants. However, we have found that there's a difference between the fee-based models of accountants and the fee-based models of the most successful wealth managers.

The fee-based models of accountants are based principally on time. The professionals in the accounting firm have an hourly or daily rate that's charged to the client and additional fees are added as incurred. The major cost is the time of the professional staff; time multiplied by the hourly rate generates the fee schedule. This is the way accountants have traditionally priced their services and the fee level is set on the basis of competitive parity or comparables – "what the market will bear." As a result, accountants generally set their rates based on what the competition is charging.

In contrast, wealth managers tend to adopt a value-based approach. Such an approach is not premised on costs or hours of effort. It's about outputs and benefits. Benefits and outputs are the result of the advice for the client as seen in the deliverables – deliverables such as an estate plan, business succession, or tax planning. And, the deliverables are central because they make tangible the value the client is getting. The financial value of the deliverable is also almost always stated as an outcome of the process (and the cost structure of delivery is taken into account). In wealth management, however, the value to the client almost always supercedes the costs, often exponentially. The client is told how much (financially) he or she will benefit. In sum, wealth management fees are tied to the perceived value to the client.

Based on our experience, value-based pricing proves to be problematic for some accountants. Value-based fees are tied more to perceived value to the client and less to the more evident cost structure of delivering the advice. To underscore that disparity, we experimented with traditional time-based versus value-based pricing at one accounting firm. A total of 20 planning cases were bid for and the pricing for all 20 cases was calculated using both approaches. Then the 20 cases were randomly divided into two groups, with one group using time-based fees and the other value-based fees.

The base cost of the value-based approach was 39.2 percent more expensive than the time-based approach. When the clients were presented with the proposals, however, the value-based presentation clearly detailed the deliverables the client would receive and the rationale for the fees. On the other hand, the time-based approach merely explained the rationale for the cost – the amount of time the accountant believed the planning would take – and explained what the client should expect.

Four out of ten of the clients who received a time-based proposal decided to go ahead with the planning compared to nine out of the ten who received the value-based proposal. Further, the clients accepting the value-based fee model generated an additional $338,000 in revenue for the accounting firm.

The moral of the story is that clients, especially the more successful and affluent ones, don't object to paying for expertise provided that they perceive that real value is being delivered. If they stand to gain by X, they understand that investing some percentage of X in the advisor makes sense. We've also found that value-based advisory fees actually engender client compliance with advisory recommendations; that is, clients who pay more for advice value it and tend to comply more readily. Further, when real value is being delivered, it enhances the quality of the relationship between the wealth manager and the client. All in all, value-based fees can be instrumental in building a stronger relationship with clients, not to mention generating significant revenues. They are indicative of the new paradigm as opposed to the current one. Finally, value-based fees help move accountants away from providing financial services and toward providing holistic financial advice in a truly consultative environment.

Creating a Wealth Management Client Pipeline

Getting clients for wealth management calls for a different mindset than that used to line up business for accounting services. Some accountants limit their thinking to clients from their client base who might benefit from certain financial and enhanced services. When they interact with those clients, they'll mention financial services and, if there's interest, they'll act. Accountants will also respond to client inquiries. Should a client ask for a particular product, the accountant can provide it. In general, much of the marketing of financial services and even wealth management services is reactive not proactive. The result is that business is generated sporadically.

For a CPA firm, the wealth management model obviously works best when there's a pipeline of clients for whom such services are beneficial. The current client roster is the place to start looking (and it may sustain many firms for some time, especially when wealth management referrals begin to roll in), but the search should not begin and end there. Before taking up prospecting, however, let's take a look at the steps involved in leveraging current client relationships.

The process starts with the wealth management platform. With the platform in place, accountants then need to understand and implement it. That in turn requires them to educate employees on how wealth management works and how to identify wealth management opportunities. This learning process can take a number of forms, and while seminars can be effective, we believe that one-on-one sessions are the best way to go about this.

An especially effective way to identifying wealth management opportunities is a process known as a *strategic scenario session*. Here the accountant works with investment management and advanced planning specialists (and sometimes a facilitator) to discuss the accountant's existing clientele as well as the people he or she is prospecting. In these sessions, a game plan is constructed for each qualified client or prospect.

For clients, the game plan will address their needs and wants as the wealth manager understands them. A modified version of the Whole Client Model™ is often used to uncover investment management and advanced planning opportunities (Exhibit 8.5). The Whole Client Model™ was developed by studying the best practices of the leading wealth managers with regard to the type of information they gather. When it comes to prospects, the *strategic scenario session* tends to focus on what and how to present. In effect, what ideas, strategies, or concepts would likely strike the right chord with the client.

EXHIBIT 8.5: The Whole Client Model™

In the Whole Client Model™, the information wealth managers gather is organized into the following six-sector framework, along with sample questions:

Goals

- What are the client's personal and professional goals?

- What does the client want – or feel obligated to do – for children, for other family members, for friends, for society, and for the world at large?

Relationships

- What family relationships (spouse, children, siblings, parents, etc.) are the most important ones in the client's personal and professional life?

- What is the client's religious orientation (and how devout is he or she)?

Assets

- How are the client's assets structured?

- How does the client make money today (and how is that likely to change in the next three years)?

Advisors

- Who are the other advisors the client is using and what role does each advisor play?

- Of late, how frequently has the client switched advisors?

Process

- How many contacts are optimal for the client each year?

- What security measures does the client use to protect personal and financial information?

Interests

- What are the client's favorite activities, TV programs, movies, and sport teams?

- Are health and fitness important to the client (and, if so, what is his or her regimen)?

Strategic scenario sessions result in numerous client wealth management opportunities being identified. The next step is a meeting with the client and, depending on the complexity of the situation, it may be wise to bring in one or more specialists. This tends to be more effective when dealing with a current client as opposed to a prospect.

Tracking a Firm's Progress

Firms that have decided to proceed with implementing a wealth management platform will want to order their activities carefully. The critical success factor approach can help them do this. Exhibit 8.6 lists the additional critical success factors necessary to implement the full transition to wealth management.

EXHIBIT 8.6: Transition Checklist

TASK AND ACTION	STATUS AND COMMENTS
Sharpen the focus on the affluent; apply consistent pressure to move upscale.	
Adopt value-based pricing.	
Create the wealth management client pipeline.	

CHAPTER 9

Wealth Management Case Studies
With Richard L. Harris

"Life is like a dogsled team. If you ain't the head dog, the scenery never changes."

LEWIS GRIZZARD

When working with any prospective client, there's a wealth management methodology that must be rigorously adhered to. Regardless of how one is ultimately paid — fees, commissions, or some combination of the two — the approach is always consultative, and that consultative methodology is governed by rules. The most important rule is clear (if sometimes difficult to uphold): the person comes first; finances and taxes second. The planning and implementation to be done is not what an accountant would do for himself or herself, nor is it meant to reflect their philosophy. It must be completely client-centric. Therefore, one needs to know as much about the client as a person as possible.

This learning process starts out with preparation: What do we already know? What clues do we have that should be followed up? The financial information and tax returns are a place to start. The returns show sources of income and lead to questions about wealth — the financial transactions that are summarized such as unearned income and sale of capital assets. Each item on the return says something about the individual, from how leveraged they are to how charitable they are.

A CPA as trusted professional will also have a history with the client. What is already known about them? What are their relationships like? What are they concerned about? What are their goals? To learn one must listen, and to understand feedback must be given to both gain affirmation and ensure that no incorrect assumptions are made prior to developing solutions.

The following cases were developed in the above manner, working with the client and the client's other advisors. The cases are broken down into two components: *Client Situation* and *Process and Results*. Although the situations are presented straightforwardly, determining the situation and developing solutions that were successfully implemented was much more complicated — complicated in that human beings and relationships are complicated.

CASE STUDY #1: Leveraging an Unneeded IRA

Client Situation: A 68-year-old widow in good health.

- She had a net worth of $30,000,000.

- She had $3,000,000 in a rollover IRA.

- She did not need the income or the principal from the IRA.

- Her children were the beneficiaries of her estate.

- She wanted part of her estate to go to her grandchildren.

- Estate taxes would be paid from the estate. Her heirs would pay $15,500,000 in estate taxes if she died plus an additional income tax of $600,000 on the IRA.

- She had not used any of her unified credit or generation skipping amount.

- She was on the board of directors of a family company and received director's fees that she reported on Schedule C of her tax return.

Process and Results: Using her Schedule C income as the basis, she set up a profit sharing plan. She contributed 20 percent of her net Schedule C income to the plan. After the plan was set up, she rolled over the IRA into the plan. The plan used $600,000 per year to purchase a $7,000,000 life insurance policy on her life.

At the same time, she set up a limited partnership. The general partnership interest was 2 percent and the limited interests were 98 percent. She funded the partnership with some of her investments. Based on appraised value, she gifted some of the limited partnership interests to the dynasty trust and some to her two children.

At the end of five years, the life insurance policy would have an approximate surrender value of $750,000, which was also about the same as the insurance policy's interpolated terminal reserve. She could either purchase the policy from the plan for $750,000 or take the policy as a distribution and pay income taxes on the

$750,000. At the same time, she would gift $750,000 to the dynasty trust. The dynasty trust would then purchase the policy from her for $750,000.

What did she accomplish?

Before:

- Her children would have inherited $29,000,000 and they would have paid estate taxes of $15,500,000 ($1,500,000 of those taxes would have been attributed to the IRA). In addition, her children would have been responsible for payment of an additional $600,000 in income taxes on the IRA.

- The IRA at $3,000,000 would have netted her children $900,000.

- Her grandchildren would have inherited $1,000,000.

Net to children	$12,900,000
Net to grandchildren	$1,000,000
Total net to family	$13,900,000
Net to taxes	$16,100,000

After:

- If she died immediately after completing the purchase of the life insurance in the profit sharing plan, her children would have inherited $26,000,000 on which they would have paid an estate tax of $13,000,000.

- The profit sharing plan would have a death benefit in the first year of $9,400,000, also going to her children. The estate tax would be $4,700,000. Only $2,400,000 would be subject to income tax, which would be $480,000.

- The grandchildren would inherit $1,000,000.

Net to children	$17,220,000
Net to grandchildren	$1,000,000
Total net to family	$18,220,000
Net to taxes	$18,180,000

If she survived more than five years and then died:

- Her children would inherit $26,000,000 on which they would pay estate taxes of $13,000,000. (We presupposed that there would be an estate tax when she dies, an assumption she agreed with.)

- The dynasty trust for the benefit of grandchildren and all future lineal descendants would receive $7,000,000 income and estate tax free.

- The dynasty trust offers a good degree of creditor protection by its terms.

Net to children	$13,000,000
Net to grandchildren	$7,000,000
Total net to family	$20,000,000
Net to taxes	$13,000,000

CASE STUDY #2: **Private Placement Life Insurance**

Client Situation: A woman had investable assets of $100,000,000.

- She used three separate professionals to manage the funds.

- All of them approached her about putting $5,000,000 into hedge funds.

- While the funds recommended had shown good historical performance and would be a good diversifier in her portfolio, the types of funds offered all had significant income tax consequences. A 12 percent rate of return net after all fees would produce a 6.85 percent return after taxes.

- The money she would use to put into the hedge funds was money that she did not and would not need to support her lifestyle.

- The funds recommended had comparable track records and the money managers were in a "beauty contest."

Process and Results: We suggested to the wealth manager we were working with that we see if wrapping the hedge fund inside a private placement life insurance policy was feasible.

The first step to see if the transaction made sense was to find out if the woman was insurable. Information about the woman's age, health, and other life insurance underwriting related issues were obtained. Based upon that, we found she would qualify for the insurance.

Next, we obtained quotes from various insurance companies committed to that marketplace, illustrating a $5,000,000 premium going to the insurance company with a 12 percent gross rate of return before related insurance costs. We asked for an illustration that would show a policy that qualified for treatment as life insurance. In qualifying as life insurance, the earnings and growth would not be subject to income tax as long as the money stayed in the policy and the policy continued to qualify as life insurance.

Because the woman did not have any present or future need for the money, we illustrated the private placement life insurance as a modified endowment contract. For income tax purposes a modified endowment life insurance contract is treated as an annuity while the insured is alive and as life insurance when the insured dies. The modified endowment contract was not an issue because there weren't any anticipated withdrawals. Creating a modified endowment contract would produce higher returns because the amount of pure life insurance in a modified endowment contract is less than that in a non-modified endowment contract policy and therefore the inherent cost inside the policy would be less.

Using proprietary comparison software, we saw that the value of the asset inside the private placement life insurance policy was approximately double the after-tax value of the hedge funds alone after 20 years. After all charges related to the private placement life insurance, the after-tax return was enhanced by more than 350 basis points. And when the woman died, the proceeds of the policy would not be subject to income tax. If she died in the early years, the insurance amount would be about twice her initial premium.

Proving the benefit of using private placement life insurance over investing personally was the first step. The second step was explaining and getting assent on the rules for the hedge fund managers regarding managing money inside the policy.

The selected insurance carrier would do due diligence, looking at among other things the track record of the managers and the investment discipline of the funds. Then the hedge fund managers would have to agree to keep this money segregated from their regular hedge fund, although it could be invested identically. The hedge fund manager was now managing a separate account for a life insurance company and was responsible for reporting to the insurance company, not the client.

The hedge fund manager saw the advantage of differentiating himself or herself in this way. The hedge fund manager went through the due diligence satisfactorily and agreed to manage that money as a separate account in a private placement life insurance policy.

CASE STUDY #3: Complexity and the Maxi-Affluent

Client Situation: Husband and wife had a $650,000,000 estate.

- He was 70 and in poor health.

- She was 66 and in excellent health.

- They had two daughters and a son.

- The son and one daughter were married, she for the second time.

- They had five grandchildren at the time.

- They spent approximately $600,000 per month to support their lifestyle.

Their assets included:

- Real estate holdings worth $400,000,000.

    These were all limited liability company interests, each property its own limited liability company.

    They were the managing members of all the limited liability companies.

    Cash flow to them was $40,000,000 per year.

- 51 percent of a manufacturing business.

    Their interest was worth about $100,000,000.

    The business was taxed as an S Corporation.

    There were voting and non-voting shares.

    They owned all the voting shares (2 percent), and the other 49 percent were non-voting shares.

    The husband was the second generation in the business.

    It was well established.

    Their interest produced $9,000,000 per year.

- Stocks, bonds and other investments worth $100,000,000. Among the assets were:

  Municipal bonds that generated $1,000,000 per year.

  Treasury bills that generated another $1,800,000 per year.

  The balance, about $50,000,000, was in stocks and some private investments.

- Personal real estate and other property worth $50,000,000.

  Among these was a vacation home worth $5,000,000.

  All the family members actively enjoyed the home.

They had done considerable planning and gifting.

- Their son and unmarried daughter owned 49 percent of the business, all non-voting interests.

  They had been responsible for a lot of the growth.

  The interest they had was considered "sweat equity" in that their parents felt they had earned it.

- All three children had trusts that each owned approximately $50,000,000 in real estate.

- They had set up a private foundation that they use for their charitable gifting.

  At the time it was worth $10,000,000.

- They had used their unified credits and generation-skipping tax exemptions.

- There was approximately $2,500,000 in trusts for their grandchildren.

- The wills provided that the surviving spouse inherited all the assets.

- At the death of the surviving spouse, $100,000,000 was to go into a testamentary charitable lead trust designed to have a zero remainder interest, with whatever actually was the remainder interest going into trusts for their children equally.

- The balance of the estate, $550,000,000 would be divided into trusts for the three children.

- The estate tax was projected to be $275,000,000.

- Based upon previous discussion with counsel:

    They were comfortable with the children receiving $275,000,000 after taxes.

    They thought that the children could raise the money for the taxes by mortgaging investment real estate and selling off personal real estate and liquid assets.

What initially got their attention was the idea that they could have as much income as they wanted, own whatever they wanted, control whatever they wanted, and have no estate tax when they died. After showing conceptually how this could be done, we were engaged to learn about them, their goals, and to give them ideas about how they could accomplish those goals.

In a series of meetings, we got to know them and their children. The children were already trustees of the family private foundation and their parents wanted them to be part of the process.

In the course of our meetings we learned:

- The parents wanted to continue to control all their assets during their lifetimes.

- They wanted to continue to live in their current lifestyle.

- They wanted a hedge against inflation.

- Their children had very close relationships with each other.

- At their deaths, they wanted the two children in the business to get control of the business.

- They wanted their other daughter to receive equal value.

- They wanted their grandchildren to have the opportunity to come into the business.

- They wanted their grandchildren and all future lineal descendants to have a sizeable asset pool.

- They wanted to protect assets going to all future generations from lawsuits, creditors, and future ex-spouses.

- They wanted to diversify their assets by selling some of their real estate.

- The real estate had low basis.

- They wanted to pay as little in income taxes as possible. However, they were willing to pay income taxes if:

   The paying of the taxes benefited their heirs, and it didn't affect their lifestyle.

- They wanted to pay as little in estate taxes as possible.

- They wanted to pay as little in generation skipping taxes as possible.

- They wanted to be remembered long after their deaths.

Process and Results: While we recommended more than was implemented, over time we did accomplish the following:

Because the husband and wife wanted to sell some of their real estate holdings and diversify, they set up a charitable remainder unitrust (CRUT). For the following reasons, the wife was the income beneficiary for her life.

- She was in excellent health.

- Her parents had lived into their 90's.

- Her husband was in poor health.

- They were willing to gamble that she would outlive him.

- The value of the remainder interest, and hence the income tax deduction, was greater than using both lives.

At her death, the remainder interest would go to their family foundation. We put real estate limited liability companies worth $100,000,000 into the charitable remainder trust. The real estate would subsequently be put up for sale and sold. Because the sale would be made by a charitable trust, no capital gains taxes had to be paid. The whole $100,000,000 was therefore available for investment. Also, because of the tax deduction created in setting up and funding the CRUT, they were able to sell another $50,000,000 of real estate personally, using the deduction to offset the gain on that sale.

Based on the husband and wife's risk tolerance, the money manager estimated that they could expect a return of 8 percent. Since they wanted a hedge against inflation, they elected a 6 percent payout from the CRUT. As the trust pays out a percent of the asset value, by paying less than the actual growth rate, the payments would increase as the asset value did. Until the real estate was sold, the income would come from the cash flow.

Additionally, based upon the same government tables, payout rates, and earnings assumptions, the foundation would get $140,000,000 in 19 years, her life expectancy (when 50 percent of the people would have died). Assuming she lived more than 19 years (past 85), she would still continue to collect the income and the amount going to the family foundation would be larger.

Next, we addressed some more items on their list:

- They wanted the business transferred to their children.

- They did not want to give up control while they were alive.

- They wanted their daughter who was not in the business to get value equal to her siblings.

- They wanted their grandchildren to have an opportunity to go into the business.

- They didn't want to pay estate taxes.

- They wanted to protect assets they transferred against lawsuits, creditors, and potential ex-spouses.

To accommodate all of the above, we set up three qualifying subchapter S trusts, one for each child. The terms of the trusts provided the asset protection the parents wanted. We sold one-third of the 49 percent non-voting interests held by the father to each of the trusts. Because they were non-voting interests in a company that lacked marketability, an appraiser determined the value to be less than the sale value of the shares if the company were sold as a whole.

But instead of a sale for cash or notes, the father took back a private annuity. This private annuity was set up to pay for his lifetime, no matter how long (or how short) he lived. Although when evaluated by insurance company underwriters his life expectancy was approximately five years, based upon regulations a government table was used to determine the payments. According to the government table his life expectancy was 16 years. Based upon that table and the earnings rate proscribed by the rules, the annual annuity payment for an interest valued before discounts at $98,000,000, was $7,500,000. This was more than covered by the actual cash flow.

This still left the father with a 2 percent interest, all of it voting. He still had control. Additionally, based upon the government regulations and tables, some of the annuity payments were considered long-term capital gains, some ordinary income, and some return of principal. When he and his wife eventually died, they would leave the voting stock as they saw fit at that time. The price of the flexibility was going to be some estate taxes (probably around $2,000,000). Although they didn't want to have any estate taxes, relative to the size of their estate and the flexibility they got in return, they thought the benefits outweighed the costs.

To handle the vacation home that the whole family used and enjoyed, we first transferred ownership of the property out of joint names and to the wife. We then set up a qualified personal residence trust with a term of 15 years. We transferred it into the wife's name because of her much greater life expectancy compared to her husband. The IRS again had regulations and a table to determine the present value of the remainder interest in the property. This time, it was based on the term of years of the trust and the interest rate used at the time. That remaining value was $1,300,000.

That remaining value was also taxable as a gift. But although gift taxes and estate taxes use the same rates, they are applied differently. If one wants to have the value of a gift in the hands of a recipient be worth $1,300,000, a gift tax of $650,000 is paid. Only the $1,300,000 that goes to the recipient is taxed. The total amount involved is $1,950,000. If one wanted someone to have $1,300,000 when they died, they would have to leave them $2,600,000. The whole $2,600,000 is taxed. Also, in this case, if the vacation property was held until death and then left to the children, the full value would be taxed. Using the same math and assuming the value had not changed, in order for the children to have the $5,000,000 vacation home free and clear, their parents would have to leave them with another $5,000,000 to pay the taxes, or if not, the children would have to personally pay $2,500,000 if it was not somehow provided.

There is another quirk involved in this transaction. According to the IRS, if the grantor of the qualified personal residence trust dies before the term of the qualified personal residence trust has expired, the full value is brought back into the estate with a credit for the gift tax previously paid. That leaves an exposure of almost $2,000,000. To protect against that possibility, the children purchased $2,000,000 of 15-year guaranteed term on their mother's life. Because of their mother's excellent health, lifestyle, and family history, she qualified for the best rates offered. The premium was $4,000 per year.

Since the parents wanted to transfer more assets to their children, we applied another technique. We set up a grantor-retained annuity trust with the wife as the annuitant. Because of a court decision that went against the IRS involving members of the Walton (Wal-Mart) family, if the grantor-retained annuity trust was properly set up, the value of the remainder interest for gift tax purposes could be zero. To accomplish that, we took $100,000,000 of non-managerial limited liability company interests and put them into the grantor retained annuity trust. An appraiser valued the interests at $65,000,000 because the interests had no control and there was no market for them.

The same rules apply to a grantor-retained annuity trust as apply to a qualified personal residence trust: if the grantor dies before the term of the grantor retained annuity trust is up, the value of the interest is brought into the estate and taxed. Because of the substantial amount at risk, we wanted to use the shortest reasonable term that we could. We had a cash flow of $10,000,000 per year to use for the annuity payments. Based upon the $65,000,000 value, the $10,000,000 annuity payment, and the government determined interest rate available, the shortest term we could use for the grantor retained annuity trust to have the value of the remainder equal zero was eight years. Again, to protect against the mother's death before the eight years was up, the children purchased $35,000,000 of 10-year guaranteed term on their mother's life for $115,000 per year.

Then we came to the grandchildren and future lineal descendants. The parents decided that if there were a way to leave them $100,000,000 with a minimal, if any tax cost, they would be interested. What we did was set up a defective dynasty trust, a trust that lasts as long as there are lineal descendants and assets. Some states have a law against perpetuities: there must be a set term measured by lives in being and 21 years, at which time the trust must end and the balance is distributed to all those eligible. Delaware does not have that law. Additionally Delaware is a state that has a lot of friendly provisions including asset protection that apply to properly drafted trusts. In order to avail them of this protection, we used a Delaware trust company as one of the co-trustees, and therefore could elect to have the trust administered in Delaware.

In following guidelines in use at the time and to accomplish our ultimate purpose, the husband and wife gifted $2,275,000 to the trust. Because that was a taxable and generation skipping gift, the taxes due were $2,850,000. Because of the ultimate result, the husband and wife paid the tax.

We then sold non-managerial real estate limited liability company interests that would have been worth $35,000,000 if the whole limited liability company were sold. They were sold for the appraised value of $22,750,000; using the same reasons for the discounts as were used in the grantor retained annuity trust transaction above. To affect the purchase, the trust gave the grantors a balloon note with interest payable at the then-current rate and the principal due at the end of 10 years. They anticipated that the principal would be paid from proceeds of a refinancing of the underlying real estate at the time it was due. They also thought the real estate value would grow by approximately 3 percent per year.

The actual annual cash flow from the limited liability company exceeded the annual interest payments by over $2,100,000. Because this was a grantor trust, the grantors personally paid whatever income taxes were due. They were willing to do that because of the fact that they had much more net-after-tax income than they needed to support their lifestyle and because by so doing, they increased what their grandchildren and future generations would receive. The $2,100,000 thus available each year was used to purchase second-to-die life insurance policies on the lives of the husband and wife. Through shopping and pitting life insurance companies against each other, despite his health and because of her health, we were able to get $70,000,000 of coverage that would be self-funded on a conservative basis after 10 years. That plus the projected value of the real estate after refinancing would total $100,000,000.

After all these transactions were done we were left with the following:

- Control of all the real estate the limited liability companies still owned.

- Control of the business.

- Liquid assets of $150,000,000.

- Income from the liquid assets of $3,000,000, a good portion non-taxable.

- Interest in real estate limited liability companies worth $115,000,000.

- Cash flow from the real estate in the limited liability company of $11,500,000.

- A business interest worth $3,000,000.

- Income from the business interest of $250,000.

- A note receivable for $22,750,000.

- Interest income from the note of $1,400,000 per year for 10 years.

- Income to the wife from the charitable remainder trust starting at $6,000,000 per year for life.

- Payments to the husband of $7,500,000 for as long as he lived from the private annuity.

- Payments of $10,000,000 per year for eight years to the wife from the grantor-retained annuity trust.

- Value transferred to the children of $203,000,000.

- Gift tax cost of transferred value of $650,000.

- Projected ultimate value of $100,000,000+ to the dynasty trust for all future lineal descendants.

- Gift and generation-skipping tax cost of $2,850,000.

- Projected ultimate value of $140,000,000 to their private foundation from the charitable remainder trust.

But we still had the rest of their estate to handle, over $350,000,000 and growing. They still thought that $325,000,000 was a reasonable number to ultimately leave to their children. And they still did not want to pay estate taxes.

At the first death of either of them, their estate went to the survivor. They changed the terms of their wills regarding the testamentary charitable lead trust. To allow for interest rate vagaries, the charitable lead trust was increased to $150,000,000. The income beneficiary was their private foundation and the remainder beneficiary a trust for their children. The terms were such that the remainder interest would be valued at zero. This plus the other techniques above achieved the desired result for the children.

The remaining voting shares they still owned in their business were left to the two children active in the business (subject to change as long as one of the parents was alive depending upon who was in the business at the time). This would result in a projected estate tax of $2,000,000 that they expected the beneficiaries to pay. The rest of their assets were left to their family foundation.

The foundation was projected to ultimately receive $600,000,000. The husband and wife knew that as long as that foundation was around, people would want to know who the people were that created it. Additionally, since their heirs would be running the foundation, they would have access and influence. And finally, as long as there were lineal descendants and assets in the dynasty trust, those descendants would want to know about the forbearers that benefited them.

Afterwords:
The Challenge of Change

Having a prescription for change is not the same thing as making a change. To achieve change at any level requires that the parties involved are confident, committed, and in complete agreement about what they have to do and how they're going to get it done. Anything less and the status quo will win the day. The willingness to take that chance means accepting the challenge of change.

In this book, we've used extensive industry research coupled with our experience working with CPA firms to show why wealth management is the wave of the future for any financial services firm that wants to connect with affluent clients and be successful. We also feel strongly that those firms that act sooner rather than later will enjoy a measurable competitive advantage.

That doesn't mean that every financial services firm, let alone every accounting firm, will wholeheartedly embrace change. Some firms will take stock of their strengths and weaknesses and decide to hold their ground at *Stage 1* with the traditional accounting model. Others will acknowledge the paradigm shift and add a financial services component, but in the end they'll be content to stop at *Stage 2*. We believe, however, that those accounting firms who are open to the challenge of change will emerge as the industry leaders.

It will not be an easy transition by any means. Even for those firms with the best intentions and the deepest resources, there will be setbacks. Partners will abandon ship, clients will lose faith, earnings will fluctuate. Still, those firms that move confidently and aggressively toward *Stage 3*, the new wealth management model, will be the ones best able to fully meet the expectations of affluent clients, guiding the accounting industry toward a new paradigm – and greater profitability.

About the Authors

RUSS ALAN PRINCE

Russ Alan Prince, president of the market research and consulting firm Prince & Associates LLC, is a leading expert on the private wealth industry on advisor-based distribution. Mr. Prince provides a variety of coaching and consulting services to professional advisors who focus on affluent markets. He is a seasoned developer of proprietary prospecting and sales and relationship management systems, and also provides high-end customized practice management programs.

DOUGLAS D. WRIGHT

Douglas D. Wright is President and Chief Operating Officer of Capital Professional Advisors, Inc., and Vice President of Enterprise Markets of CPA2Biz. Capital Professional Advisors, Inc., a CPA2Biz company, was established in 1999 by Mr. Wright and some of the largest accounting firms in the country to help mature, middle-market CPA firms expand their service offerings and take their businesses to a new level. CPA2Biz was developed by CPAs for CPAs, their clients and employers as a comprehensive provider of tools, resources, value-added services and application solutions that strengthen and add value to the relationships between CPAs and the organizations they serve. In 2000 and 2001, he was named one of the 100 most influential people in the accounting profession by *Accounting Today* and was identified by the same publication as one of the top ten people to watch in financial services.

RICHARD C. URBEALIS

Richard C. Urbealis was Sr. VP, National Business Advisor for Capital Professional Advisors, Inc. ("Capital"). He currently manages a successful consulting firm, Compass Professional Advisors, that provides services to Capital and other firms and individuals seeking to develop alternative distribution strategies. Mr. Urbealis has consulted with hundreds of accounting firms across the country on the topic of financial services as a practice area. He is recognized as an expert of trends affecting the public accounting profession, such as the recent massive consolidation of the industry, changing regulatory climate, financial service integration and information technology integration. Mr. Urbealis is a popular speaker to public accounting groups and is frequently asked to lead strategic planning efforts of some of America's leading accounting firms.

RICHARD L. HARRIS

richard@bpnmont.com

Richard L. Harris is the managing member of BPN Montaigne LLC, a firm devoted to working with accountants and their affluent clients advising on wealth enhancement, wealth transfer, asset protection, and philanthropic planning. Mr. Harris is known for his integrity and creativity as a problem solver for accountants and their very rich clients. He specializes in custom-crafted solutions that take into account personal desires, concerns, and financial complexities. In conjunction with his advisory board and professional network, he brings together expertise and cutting-edge ideas to craft scenarios that integrate and address the issues at hand. Mr. Harris has worked with accountants for over thirty years, serving in part as a back office providing advanced planning concepts, products, and second opinions – as well as running educational seminars. He is the co-author of *Advanced Planning with the Ultra-Affluent: A Framework for Professional Advisors,* published in 2002 by Private Asset Management - Institutional Investor, Inc.